SRA Spelling

Dr. Nancy L. Roser
Professor, Language and Literacy Studies
The University of Texas
College of Education
Austin, Texas

Dr. Jean Wallace Gillet
Reading Specialist
Charlottesville Public Schools
Charlottesville, VA

**SRA
McGraw-Hill**

Columbus, Ohio

A Division of The McGraw·Hill Companies

Program Reviewers

Wendy Fries
Teacher GATE Coordinator
Kings River Union School District
Kingsburg, CA

Cynthia W. Gardner
Exceptional Children's Teacher
Balls Creek Elementary School
Newton, NC

Diane Jones
Teacher
East Clayton Elementary School
Clayton, NC

Sheryl Kurtin
Curriculum Teacher
Tuttle Elementary School
Sarasota, FL

Ann Ogburn
Curriculum Coordinator
Johnston County Schools
Smithfield, NC

Michael Reck
Teacher
Big Walnut Schools
Sunbury, OH

Dr. Sherry V. Reynolds
Classroom Teacher/Elementary
 Curriculum Specialist
Will Rogers Elementary School
Stillwater, OK

Cover Photos: tl STUDIOHIO, **tr** Aaron Haupt, **bc** Paul Chauncey/The
br George Schiavone/The Stock Market.

Illustrations: Steve McInturff

Electronic Illustrations: Jennie Copeland, Tom Goodwin

www.sra4kids.com

SRA/McGraw-Hill

A Division of The McGraw·Hill Companies

Send all inquiries to:
SRA/McGraw-Hill
4400 Easton Commons
Columbus, OH 43219

Printed in the United States of America.

ISBN 0-07-572287-9

8 9 10 QPD 0 9 8

How to Study a Word

1 **Look** at the word.   **print**
What does it mean?
How is it spelled?

2 **Say** the word.   **print**
What sounds do you hear?
Are there any silent letters?

3 **Think** about the word.   **pr i nt**
How is each sound spelled?
Do you see any word parts?

4 **Write** the word.   **print**
Did you copy all the letters
  carefully?
Did you think about the sounds
  and letters?

5 **Check** the spelling.   **print**
Did you spell the word correctly?
Do you need to write it again?

Contents

1 The /a/ Sound

Spelling Focus—The /a/ sound can be spelled *a*.

 RHYMING STRATEGY Write the Core Words that rhyme with the following words.

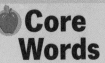 **Core Words**

1. lap
2. hat
3. man
4. ram
5. bad
6. map
7. pat
8. mad
9. jam
10. gas

My Words

Core Word Sentences

The book is on her **lap.**

Put the **hat** on your head.

That **man** is smart.

The firemen used a **ram.**

I feel **bad** about going.

Find the city on the **map.**

I **pat** the dog on its head.

Losing makes him **mad.**

Put **jam** on the bread.

Fill the tank with **gas.**

dad

1. _____

2. _____

dam

1. _____

2. _____

cat

1. _____

2. _____

tap

1. _____

2. _____

lass

1. _____

fan

1. _____

WRITE Write a sentence for each Core Word on a separate sheet of paper.

MEANING STRATEGY Write the Core Words that best complete the story. Use each word only once.

What a Day!

REST STOP
8,000 MILES

MAP

One day in the park, I saw a _____ sitting on a

bench. He had a tall, red _____ on his head. He

was eating bread and _____. He had a road

_____ on his _____. A white

_____ was standing next to him. The ram's name

was Sam. I wanted to _____ Sam the ram.

The man looked _____. It was a very

_____ day for him. His car was out of

_____, and he had to walk all the way home.

Core Words
1. lap
2. hat
3. man
4. ram
5. bad
6. map
7. pat
8. mad
9. jam
10. gas

Challenge Words
as
has
path
dash
cash

PRONUNCIATION STRATEGY Add the missing vowel to write the Core Words. Say the word.

1. l _ p _____
2. m _ p _____
3. h _ t _____
4. p _ t _____
5. g _ s _____
6. m _ d _____
7. b _ d _____
8. r _ m _____
9. j _ m _____
10. m _ n _____

RHYMING STRATEGY Write two rhyming pairs of Challenge Words.

1. _____ _____

2. _____ _____

Write the Challenge Word that rhymes with *bath.*

3. _____

PROOFREADING STRATEGY Here is a draft of one student's story about a bad day. Find three misspelled Core Words. Circle them and write them correctly.

Proofreading Marks

⬭	misspelling
⊙	add a period
═	make a capital letter

Monday was a bed day. I spilled milk on my lup. After that, I sat on my new hat. Then I could not find the state I live in on the mep. I was sad that day.

1. _____

2. _____

3. _____

 MEANING STRATEGY Story
Plan to write a story about a bad day that you had. Think about all the things that went wrong during your bad day. Choose and write at least three Core Words that you will use in your story. Write your story on a separate sheet of paper.

1. _____   2. _____   3. _____

Now proofread your word list and story and correct any errors.

2 The /i/ Sound

Spelling Focus—The /i/ sound can be spelled *i*.

Core Words

1. if
2. zip
3. mix
4. pin
5. milk
6. tip
7. his
8. fix
9. kiss
10. rip

My Words

 RHYMING STRATEGY Write the Core Words that rhyme with the following words.

Core Word Sentences

I'll be glad **if** you come.
What is the **zip** code?
I will **mix** the ingredients.
Put the **pin** on your shirt.
Pour **milk** on the cereal.
Don't **tip** over the boat!
He does **his** homework.
Can you **fix** the radio?
She will **kiss** the baby.
Don't **rip** the paper.

win

1. _____

is

1. _____

lip

1. _____

2. _____

3. _____

stiff

1. _____

six

1. _____

2. _____

silk

1. _____

hiss

1. _____

WRITE Write a sentence for each Core Word on a separate sheet of paper.

MEANING STRATEGY Write the Core Words that best complete the story. Use each word only once.

A Real Treat

Josh decided to _____ his mom a salad for lunch.

He had to _____ the leaves off a head of lettuce. He cut

off the end, or _____, of a carrot. He had to _____ the

oil and vinegar for the salad dressing. He poured _____

mom a glass of _____. Then Josh tried to _____

a note on his mom's napkin. He found some paper in his

backpack. He remembered to _____ up the backpack

when he was done. His mom gave him a big _____.

You could make your mother lunch _____ you tried.

Core Words

1. if
2. zip
3. mix
4. pin
5. milk
6. tip
7. his
8. fix
9. kiss
10. rip

Challenge Words

dish
fish
wish
mitt
rich

VISUALIZATION STRATEGY Change one letter in each word to write a Core Word.

1. zap _____

2. top _____

3. rap _____

4. pan _____

5. of _____

6. fox _____

7. has _____

8. silk _____

9. fix _____

RHYMING STRATEGY Write the Challenge Words that fit these clues.

1. They end in -ish.

_____

_____

_____

2. It rhymes with kit.

_____

3. It rhymes with which.

_____

PROOFREADING STRATEGY Here is a draft of one student's list of nice things to do for someone. Find three misspelled Core Words. Circle them and write them correctly.

Proofreading Marks

⬭ misspelling

⊙ add a period

= make a capital letter

1. Try to fex a broken toy.
2. Play a game ef I have time.
3. Give a hug and a kis.

1. _____

2. _____

3. _____

MEANING STRATEGY List
Plan to make a list of things you can do for someone you like. Think of things you might do to please someone you know. Choose and write at least three Core Words that you will use in your list. Write your list on a separate sheet of paper.

1. _____   2. _____   3. _____

Now proofread your word list and "things to do" list and correct any errors.

3 The /o/ and /ô/ Sounds

Spelling Focus—The /o/ and /ô/ sounds can be spelled o.

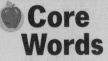 **Core Words**

1. cot
2. fog
3. lot
4. log
5. got
6. dog
7. flop
8. jog
9. job
10. spot

My Words

RHYMING STRATEGY Write the Core Words that rhyme with the following words.

Core Word Sentences

Sleep on the **cot.**

The **fog** hid the plane.

The house is on a big **lot.**

Saw the **log** into boards.

I've **got** a sore finger.

The **dog** barked.

The dog's ears **flop.**

I can **jog** ten miles.

He was hired for the **job.**

I can **spot** a faraway bird.

tot

1. _____

2. _____

3. _____

4. _____

bog

1. _____

2. _____

3. _____

4. _____

sob

1. _____

top

1. _____

 WRITE Write a sentence for each Core Word on a separate sheet of paper.

MEANING STRATEGY Write the Core Words that best complete the story. Use each word only once.

A Great Job

Meg _____ a new after-school _____.

Meg's job is a _____ of fun. She takes a big

_____ for walks. She has to take the dog out every

day in sun, rain, or _____.

Sometimes Meg takes the dog to a safe _____. It

runs around while Meg takes a _____. Other times

she likes to _____ down on a _____ while

the dog runs around by itself. Then they both go home and

rest on a _____.

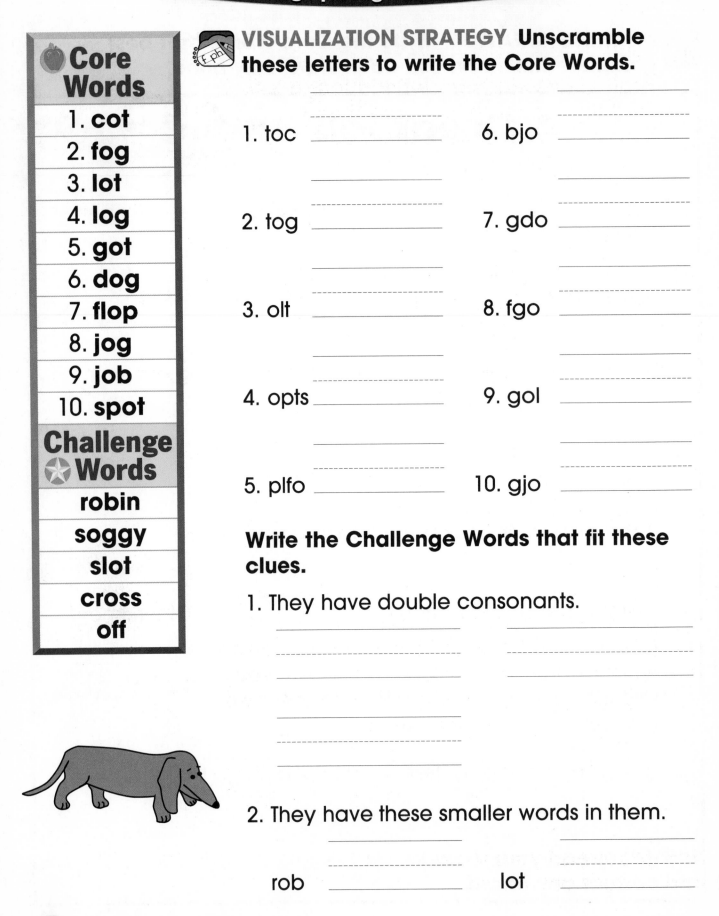

Core Words

1. **cot**
2. **fog**
3. **lot**
4. **log**
5. **got**
6. **dog**
7. **flop**
8. **jog**
9. **job**
10. **spot**

Challenge Words

robin

soggy

slot

cross

off

VISUALIZATION STRATEGY Unscramble these letters to write the Core Words.

1. toc _____

2. tog _____

3. olt _____

4. opts _____

5. plfo _____

6. bjo _____

7. gdo _____

8. fgo _____

9. gol _____

10. gjo _____

Write the Challenge Words that fit these clues.

1. They have double consonants.

_____   _____

_____

2. They have these smaller words in them.

rob _____   lot _____

Proofreading and Writing

PROOFREADING STRATEGY Here is a draft of one student's letter about a job. Find three misspelled Core Words. Circle them and write them correctly.

Proofreading Marks

⬭ misspelling

⊙ add a period

= make a capital letter

Dear Rose,

   I got a jeb. It is a lat of work. I wash our dog. I get off every spat of dirt. My family likes my work. So does my dog.

     Your friend,

     Dan

1. _____

2. _____

3. _____

 MEANING STRATEGY Letter
Plan to write a letter to a friend about a job you would like. Think of the kind of job you would like to have. Choose and write at least three Core Words that you will use in your letter. Write your letter on a separate sheet of paper.

1. _____ 2. _____ 3. _____

Now proofread your word list and letter and correct any errors.

Unit 1 • Lesson 3   13

4 The Final /k/ Sound

Spelling Focus—The final /k/ sound can be spelled *ck*. The *ck* spelling is usually found at the end of a word.

 **PRONUNCIATION STRATEGY** Say the Core Words. Write the ones that end with the following letters.

Core Words

1. dock
2. snack
3. lock
4. pack
5. sick
6. rock
7. sack
8. stick
9. stack
10. kick

My Words

Core Word Sentences

The boat left the **dock.**

Don't **snack** between meals.

The key fit the **lock.**

I'll **pack** the suitcase.

Germs make us **sick.**

Don't **rock** the boat.

He filled the **sack** with flour.

The stamp does not **stick.**

Dry that **stack** of dishes.

She will **kick** the football.

ick

4. _____

1. _____

2. _____

3. _____

ack

1. _____

2. _____

3. _____

ock

1. _____

2. _____

3. _____

MEANING STRATEGY Write the Core Words that best complete the story. Use each word only once.

A Busy Afternoon

I like to go to the boat _____ with my friend.

We climb the big _____ on the shore. I use a walking

_____ to help me walk up the rock. Once there, we

_____ on apples and nuts. My friend and I

_____ the food in a paper _____. There is a lot of

trash on the dock. It makes me _____! I _____

a can with almost every step! My friend and I _____

the trash in a pile and take it to the dump. We have to get

there before they _____ the gates at five o'clock.

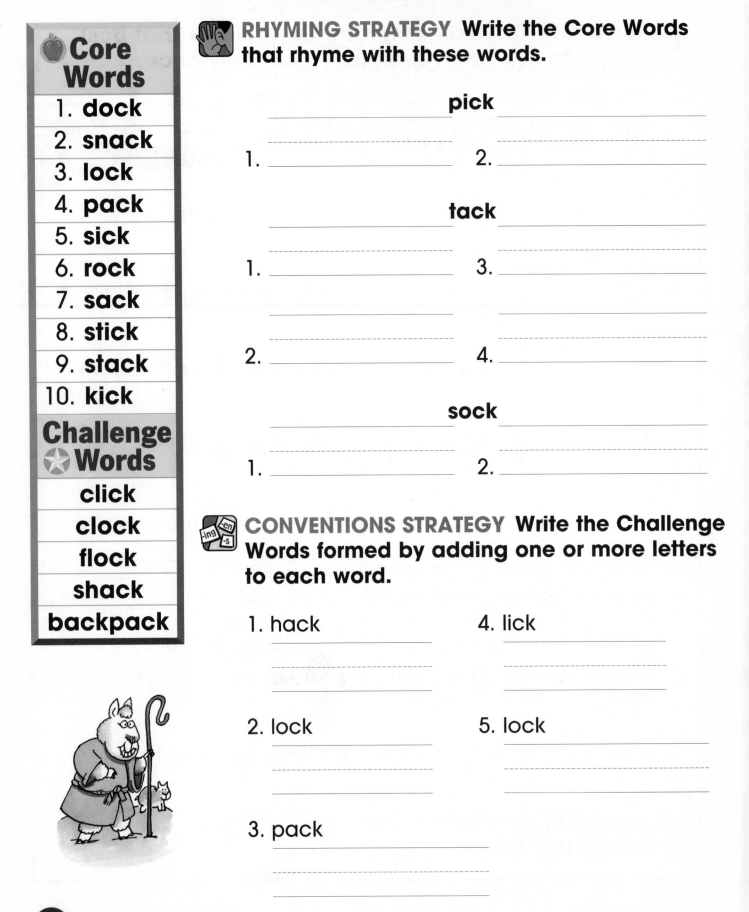

Core Words

1. dock
2. snack
3. lock
4. pack
5. sick
6. rock
7. sack
8. stick
9. stack
10. kick

Challenge Words

click
clock
flock
shack
backpack

RHYMING STRATEGY Write the Core Words that rhyme with these words.

pick

1. _____   2. _____

tack

1. _____   3. _____

2. _____   4. _____

sock

1. _____   2. _____

CONVENTIONS STRATEGY Write the Challenge Words formed by adding one or more letters to each word.

1. hack _____

2. lock _____

3. pack _____

4. lick _____

5. lock _____

PROOFREADING STRATEGY Here is a draft of one student's list of things to do. Find three misspelled Core Words. Circle them and write them correctly.

Proofreading Marks

⬭	misspelling
⊙	add a period
=	make a capital letter

Things I Like to Do
1. Kik a football.
2. Hit a ball with a stik.
3. Fish off the dok.
4. Climb a rock.

1. _____

2. _____

3. _____

 MEANING STRATEGY List
Plan to make a list of things you like to do after school. Think of the things that are the most fun to do. Choose and write at least three Core Words that you will use in your list. Write your list on a separate sheet of paper.

1. _____   2. _____   3. _____

Now proofread your word list and "to do" list and correct any errors.

5 The /nd/ and /st/ Sounds

Spelling Focus—The /nd/ sound can be spelled *nd*. The /st/ sound can be spelled *st*. nd is never found at the beginning of a word.

PRONUNCIATION STRATEGY
Say each Core Word. Write the Core Words with the following spellings.

Core Word Sentences

The frog lives in the **pond.**
The bus **just** left.
I play in the school **band.**
This show will **last** an hour.
She put **sand** in the pail.
Write the words in a **list.**
I **lost** my left glove.
Hold the pen in your **hand.**
How **fast** can you run?
The cat **and** dog played.

Core Words

1. pond
2. just
3. band
4. last
5. sand
6. list
7. lost
8. hand
9. fast
10. and

My Words

nd

1. _____
2. _____

st

3. _____
4. _____
5. _____

1. _____
2. _____
3. _____
4. _____
5. _____

MEANING STRATEGY Write the Core Words that best complete the story. Use each word only once.

My Lost Cat

I cannot find my cat, Fluffy. She is _____ .

I saw her _____ this morning. Fluffy and I were near

the fish _____ in my backyard. I was digging in the

_____ . She was sitting next to me. I held out my

_____ . "Here, Fluffy!" I called. But she ran away as

_____ as she could. That was the _____

time I saw her. She has a white _____ around her

neck _____ a white tail. I made a _____

of places to look for her. I miss my pet!

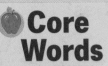
Core Words

1. **pond**
2. **just**
3. **band**
4. **last**
5. **sand**
6. **list**
7. **lost**
8. **hand**
9. **fast**
10. **and**

Challenge Words

cast
past
land
stand
wind

 CONSONANT-SUBSTITUTION STRATEGY
Do these word problems. Then write the Core Words.

1. j + dust – d =

2. f + mast – m =

3. l + past – p =

4. ant – t + d =

5. l + mist – m =

6. s + land – l =

7. h + band – b =

8. p + fond – f =

 VISUALIZATION STRATEGY Add the underlined word parts together to make Challenge Words.

1. s<u>aw</u> + w<u>indow</u> =

2. <u>st</u>op + h<u>and</u> =

3. <u>l</u>aw + h<u>and</u> =

4. <u>can</u> + <u>st</u>ar =

5. <u>pass</u> + <u>t</u>op =

PROOFREADING STRATEGY Here is a draft of one student's poster about a lost horse. Find three misspelled Core Words. Circle them and write them correctly.

Proofreading Marks
⬭ misspelling
⊙ add a period
＝ make a capital letter

> PLEASE HELP!
> Have you seen Toby? He is lawst. He is a brown horse. He has a white bandd down his back. Toby was last seen near the pend.

1. _____

2. _____

3. _____

 MEANING STRATEGY Poster

Plan to make a poster telling about something that you lost. Think of the pictures and words you might put on your poster. Choose and write at least three Core Words that you will use on your poster. Write the words for your poster on a separate sheet of paper.

1. _____   2. _____   3. _____

Now proofread your word list and poster and correct any errors.

Lesson 1

Lesson 1

man
ram
pat
bad
lap
jam

RHYMING STRATEGY Write two Core Words that spell the /a/ sound and rhyme with *ham.*

1. _____   2. _____

MEANING STRATEGY Write a Core Word for each clue.

3. A cat might sit here. _____

4. A boy will grow up to become this. _____

Lesson 2

Lesson 2

his
pin
tip
kiss
mix
zip

RHYMING STRATEGY Write two Core Words that spell the /i/ sound and rhyme with *lip.*

1. _____   2. _____

MEANING STRATEGY Write a Core Word that fits each group of words.

3. needle, thread, _____   4. hers, yours, _____

CONVENTIONS STRATEGY Write the Core Words formed by dropping one or more letters from each word.

5. mixes _____   6. kissing _____

Review

Lesson 3

job
cot
fog
log
dog
lot

RHYMING STRATEGY Write two Core Words that spell the /o/ sound and rhyme with *got.*

1. _____

2. _____

VOWEL-SUBSTITUTION STRATEGY Change one letter in each word to write a Core Word.

3. leg _____

4. jab _____

Lesson 4

Lesson 4

stack
pack
kick
rock
sick
dock

RHYMING STRATEGY Write two Core Words that spell the /k/ sound and rhyme with *back.*

1. _____

2. _____

MEANING STRATEGY Write a Core Word that fits each clue.

3. boat, ship, _____

4. stone, pebble, _____

RHYMING STRATEGY Write the Core Words that rhyme with this word.

5. lick _____ _____

Review

Lesson 5

fast
hand
pond
last
list
lost

PRONUNCIATION STRATEGY Say each Core Word. Write two Core Words that spell the /nd/ sound.

1. _____   2. _____

MEANING STRATEGY Write a Core Word that is an antonym, or opposite, for each word.

3. found _____   4. first _____

VISUALIZATION STRATEGY Unscramble these letters to write the Core Words.

5. stli _____   6. stfa _____

Spelling Strategy

THINK Look at the Core Word lists on pages 22–24. Choose two words that are the hardest for you to spell. Write the words and a strategy to help you remember how to spell each word.

Words	Spelling Strategies
1.	
2.	

Review

 PROOFREADING STRATEGY Read the story. Find three misspelled Core Words. Circle them and write them correctly.

Beth gott her own breakfast. she had a glass of malk. She had toast with peanut butter and jamm. Then beth ate an orange. Her cat had some milk.

	Proofreading Marks
⬭	misspelling
═	make a capital letter
⊙	add a period

1. _____

2. _____

3. _____

Now find two words that should begin with a capital letter. Underline each letter three times to show it should be a capital letter.

MEANING STRATEGY Poem
Write a poem that tells about a brave or kind deed. Use at least four spelling words. First, write the spelling words that you want to use.

1. _____

2. _____

3. _____

4. _____

Now proofread your words and poem and correct any errors.

Review

 **SPELLING FUN** Use these Core Words from Lessons 1–5 to complete the puzzle.

Lesson 1

map

gas

Lesson 2

milk

if

fix

rip

mix

Lesson 3

fog

flop

Lesson 4

lock

rock

snack

stick

Lesson 5

sand

band

ACROSS

2. Mist
5. Blend together
6. Food between meals
7. I will help you _____ you help me.
9. Use a bucket and shovel with this.
10. Has its own key
11. Tear
12. Use this to find the location of things.

DOWN

1. Hard as a _____
2. Mend or repair
3. Fuel for car
4. Strike up the _____ .
5. Something you drink
8. To flap loosely
9. Piece of thin wood

26 **Lesson 6 Review**

Review
STANDARDIZED-FORMAT TEST PRACTICE

Choose the correct spelling of the Core Words from Lessons 1–5.

ANSWERS

SAMPLE	A. gott	B. gout	C. got	Ⓐ Ⓑ ⓒ
1.	A. dag	B. dawg	C. dog	Ⓐ Ⓑ Ⓒ
2.	A. juste	B. just	C. jeust	Ⓐ Ⓑ Ⓒ
3.	A. kiss	B. kis	C. ciss	Ⓐ Ⓑ Ⓒ
4.	A. stik	B. stic	C. stick	Ⓐ Ⓑ Ⓒ

Choose the misspelled Core Words from Lessons 1–5.

SAMPLE	A. map	B. tipp	C. gas	Ⓐ Ⓑ Ⓒ
1.	A. and	B. madd	C. jog	Ⓐ Ⓑ Ⓒ
2.	A. kick	B. last	C. lawg	Ⓐ Ⓑ Ⓒ
3.	A. iff	B. hat	C. sack	Ⓐ Ⓑ Ⓒ
4.	A. spott	B. pin	C. pat	Ⓐ Ⓑ Ⓒ

Choose the correct spelling of the Core Words from Lessons 1–5 to complete each sentence.

SAMPLE	We got _____ in the woods.			
	A. lawst	B. loste	C. lost	Ⓐ Ⓑ ⓒ

1. Make sure you _____ the door.
   A. loc   B. lock   C. loch   Ⓐ Ⓑ Ⓒ

2. We swam in the _____.
   A. pand   B. pont   C. pond   Ⓐ Ⓑ Ⓒ

3. I had a _____ day.
   A. badd   B. baad   C. bad   Ⓐ Ⓑ Ⓒ

4. That is _____ hat.
   A. hiz   B. hizz   C. his   Ⓐ Ⓑ Ⓒ

7 The /e/ Sound

Spelling Focus—The /e/ sound can be spelled *e*.

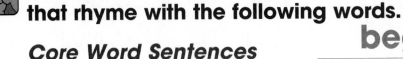 **RHYMING STRATEGY** Write the Core Words that rhyme with the following words.

🍎 Core Words

1. egg
2. fed
3. met
4. yet
5. went
6. nest
7. rest
8. test
9. bend
10. send

My Words

Core Word Sentences

I saw the chick and the **egg.**
The bird **fed** the chicks.
I **met** a friend at the mall.
Are you ready **yet?**
He **went** home early.
The robin built a **nest.**
Take the **rest** of the candy.
I passed the **test.**
Here's a **bend** in the road.
You can **send** a letter.

beg

1. _____

bed

1. _____

lend

1. _____

2. _____

let

1. _____

2. _____

sent

1. _____

best

1. _____

2. _____

3. _____

🍎 **WRITE** Write a sentence for each Core Word on a separate sheet of paper.

MEANING STRATEGY Write the Core Words that best complete the letter. Use each word only once.

Dear Uncle Bill

Dear Uncle Bill,

_____

A robin built a _____ in our yard.

_____

Soon a tiny _____ hatched. The baby poked its head

_____

out and _____ its mother. The mother did not sit and

_____   _____

_____. She _____ away and came back

_____   _____

and _____ the baby a worm. She had to _____

down to feed it. The baby robin cannot leave the nest

_____   _____

_____. Someday it will _____ its wings

_____

and try to fly. I will _____ you a picture of the robins.

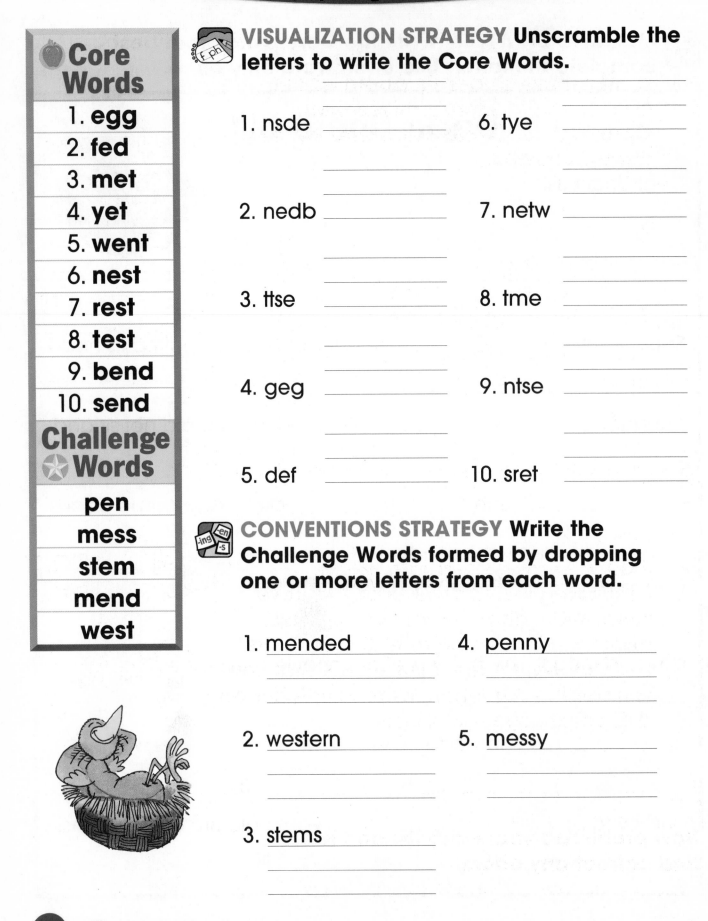

Core Words

1. **egg**
2. **fed**
3. **met**
4. **yet**
5. **went**
6. **nest**
7. **rest**
8. **test**
9. **bend**
10. **send**

Challenge Words

pen

mess

stem

mend

west

VISUALIZATION STRATEGY Unscramble the letters to write the Core Words.

1. nsde _____

2. nedb _____

3. ttse _____

4. geg _____

5. def _____

6. tye _____

7. netw _____

8. tme _____

9. ntse _____

10. sret _____

CONVENTIONS STRATEGY Write the Challenge Words formed by dropping one or more letters from each word.

1. mended _____

2. western _____

3. stems _____

4. penny _____

5. messy _____

PROOFREADING STRATEGY Here is a draft of one student's poem about blue jays. Find three misspelled Core Words. Circle them and write them correctly.

Proofreading Marks

⬭ misspelling

⊙ add a period

= make a capital letter

I mat some little blue jays,
So I gave them all some hay.
They built a small and cozy nast.
They worked hard and did
not rist!

1. _____

2. _____

3. _____

MEANING STRATEGY Friendly Letter
Plan to write a letter to a friend describing a bird or animal you have seen. Think about what you noticed about the bird or animal. Choose and write at least three Core Words that you will use in your letter. Write your letter on a separate sheet of paper.

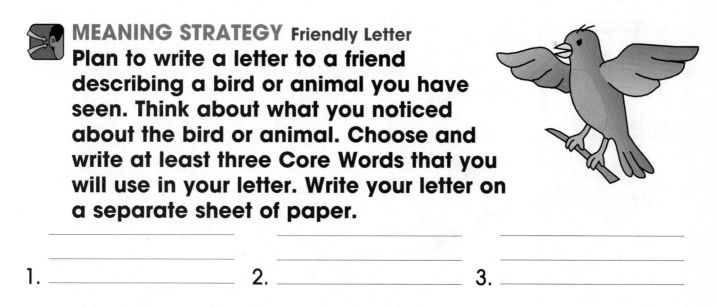

1. _____ 2. _____ 3. _____

Now proofread your word list and letter and correct any errors.

8 The /u/ Sound

Spelling Focus—The /u/ sound can be spelled *u*.

 Core Words

1. us
2. mud
3. rub
4. rust
5. tug
6. luck
7. must
8. rug
9. shut
10. stuck

My Words

_____

_____

_____

_____

_____

_____

_____

_____

RHYMING STRATEGY Write the Core Words that rhyme with the following words.

Core Word Sentences

The man thanked **us.**
There was **mud** on our shoes.
I will **rub** the magic lamp.
That metal will **rust.**
The dog will **tug** the leash.
Good **luck** with your work!
We **must** go home early.
The **rug** covered the floor.
Please **shut** the door.
She **stuck** out her tongue.

tub
1. _____

bus
1. _____

buck
1. _____

2. _____

cud
1. _____

lug
1. _____

2. _____

dust
1. _____

hut
1. _____
2. _____

 WRITE Write a sentence for each Core Word on a separate sheet of paper.

MEANING STRATEGY Write the Core Words that best complete the story. Use each word only once.

Car Wash

Every Saturday my sister and I _____

_____

wash our family car. We wash off the dirt and _____.

We always make sure to _____ the windows so the

inside stays dry. Sometimes we find some _____ on the

car. It will not _____ off. We shake the sand from the

_____

_____ on the floor. Sometimes the seat gets

_____

_____. One good _____ is all it takes to move it.

With _____ we can finish the job in an hour. It

makes _____ feel good when the job is done.

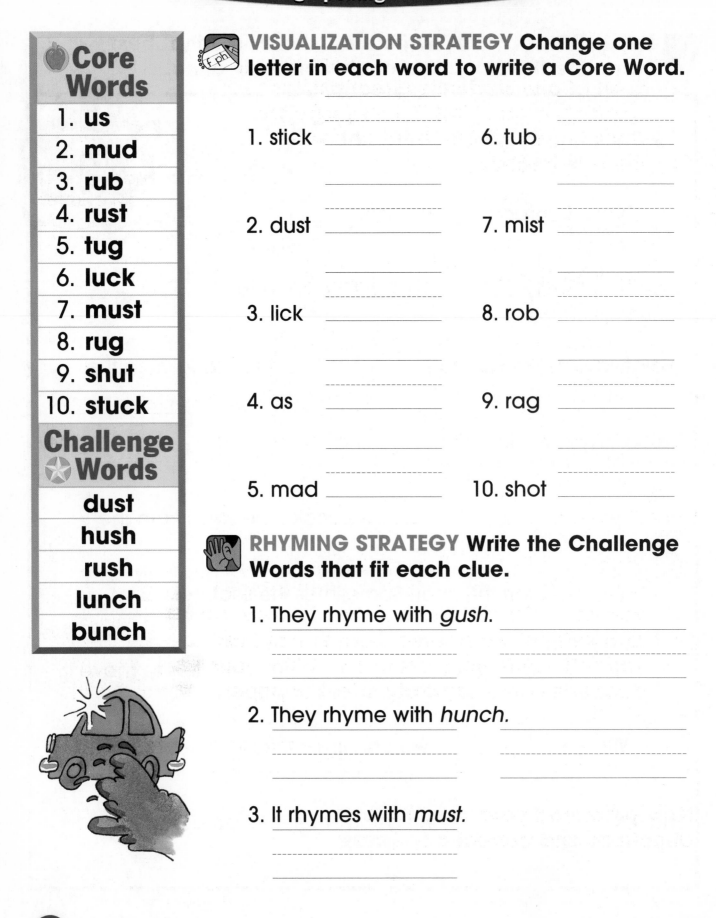

Core Words

1. us
2. mud
3. rub
4. rust
5. tug
6. luck
7. must
8. rug
9. shut
10. stuck

Challenge Words

dust
hush
rush
lunch
bunch

VISUALIZATION STRATEGY Change one letter in each word to write a Core Word.

1. stick _____   6. tub _____

2. dust _____   7. mist _____

3. lick _____   8. rob _____

4. as _____   9. rag _____

5. mad _____   10. shot _____

RHYMING STRATEGY Write the Challenge Words that fit each clue.

1. They rhyme with *gush.*

2. They rhyme with *hunch.*

3. It rhymes with *must.*

PROOFREADING STRATEGY Here is a draft of one student's directions for washing a car. Find three misspelled Core Words. Circle them and write them correctly.

Proofreading Marks

⬭	misspelling
⊙	add a period
=	make a capital letter

1. Shet the doors and close the windows.
2. Wash the car and rob with a rag.
3. Shake the dirt from the rog.

1. _____

2. _____

3. _____

 MEANING STRATEGY Directions

Plan to write directions telling how to wash a car. Think of the different things you do when you wash a car. Choose and write at least three Core Words that you will use in your directions. Write your directions on a separate sheet of paper.

1. _____   2. _____   3. _____

Now proofread your word list and directions and correct any errors.

9 Words with *gr*, *dr*, and *tr*

Spelling Focus—The /gr/ sound can be spelled *gr*. The /dr/ sound can be spelled *dr*. The /tr/ sound can be spelled *tr*.

🍎 Core Words

1. grand
2. drum
3. tree
4. drove
5. grin
6. truck
7. drip
8. trip
9. drive
10. gray

My Words

_____

_____

_____

_____

_____

_____

PRONUNCIATION STRATEGY
Write the Core Words with the following spellings.

Core Word Sentences

Birthdays are **grand** fun.

Beat the **drum.**

Climb the oak **tree.**

Dad **drove** the car.

I **grin** when I'm happy.

The **truck** turned left.

A leaky faucet will **drip.**

Don't **trip** on the rocks.

That cat may **drive** me crazy.

My coat is **gray.**

dr

1. _____

2. _____

3. _____

4. _____

gr

1. _____

2. _____

3. _____

tr

1. _____

2. _____

3. _____

🍎 **WRITE** Write a sentence for each Core Word on a separate sheet of paper.

MEANING STRATEGY Write the Core Words that best complete the story. Use each word only once.

The Family Truck

Mal's family owns a pickup _____. It is painted

_____. They park it under a shady _____. Mal

wants to _____ a truck just like it someday.

One day oil began to _____ from it, so the truck

had to be fixed.

Last summer Mal went with his family on a _____.

They _____ a long way to see some friends. They gave

Mal a big _____. Mal gave them a big _____

in return. He thought his drum was _____!

Core Words

1. **grand**
2. **drum**
3. **tree**
4. **drove**
5. **grin**
6. **truck**
7. **drip**
8. **trip**
9. **drive**
10. **gray**

Challenge Words

dress
trim
try
grass
grow

VISUALIZATION STRATEGY Change one letter in each word to write a Core Word.

1. trick _____

2. free _____

3. trip _____

4. dram _____

5. drove _____

6. tray _____

7. grip _____

8. drive _____

9. brand _____

10. drip _____

PRONUNCIATION STRATEGY Say each Challenge Word. Write the one that has the same vowel as the given word.

1. him _____

2. show _____

3. less _____

4. pass _____

5. my _____

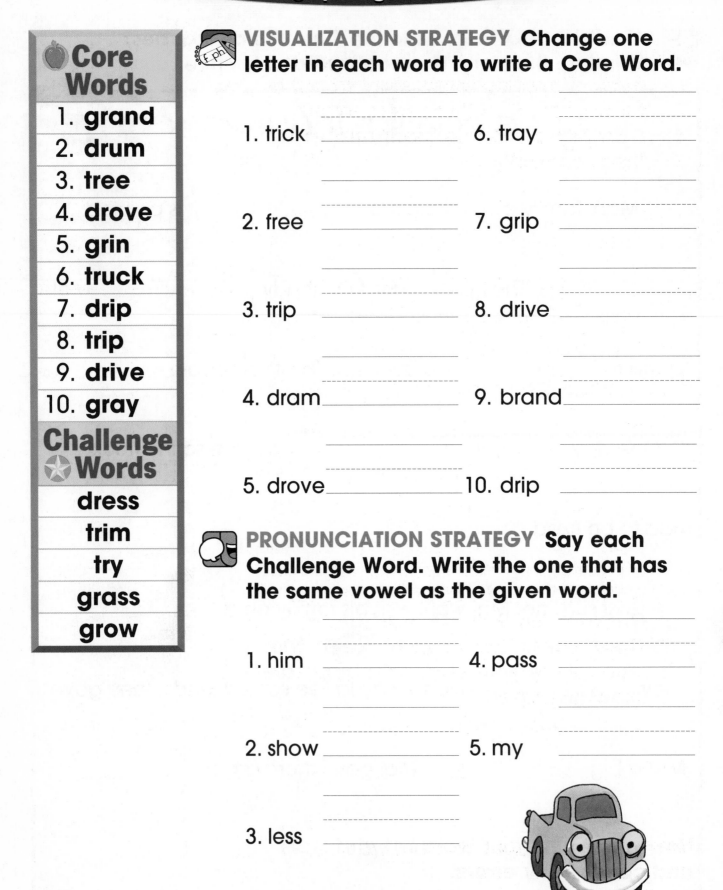

PROOFREADING STRATEGY Here is a draft of one student's story about a family trip. Find three misspelled Core Words. Circle them and write them correctly.

Proofreading Marks

⬭	misspelling
⊙	add a period
═	make a capital letter

Last summer my family took a trap. We had a grond time. We drov to the lake. It was a long drive, but we had lots of fun.

1. _____

2. _____

3. _____

MEANING STRATEGY Story
Plan to write a story about a trip you have taken. Think about where you went and what happened to you. Choose and write at least three Core Words that you will use in your story. Write your story on a separate sheet of paper.

1. _____ 2. _____ 3. _____

Now proofread your word list and story and correct any errors.

10 Words with *gl*, *bl*, and *pl*

***Spelling Focus*—The /bl/ sound can be spelled *bl*. The /gl/ sound can be spelled *gl*. The /pl/ sound can be spelled *pl*.**

🍎 Core Words

1. plus
2. glass
3. blink
4. plot
5. glad
6. blend
7. plan
8. block
9. plum
10. blast

My Words

PRONUNCIATION STRATEGY
Say each Core Word. Write the words with the following spellings.

Core Word Sentences

Two **plus** two is four.

Have a **glass** of milk.

Do not **blink** your eyes.

The story has a good **plot.**

I am **glad** you came.

I will **blend** the cake mix.

I am going to **plan** a party.

He won't **block** your way.

The **plum** was juicy.

The **blast** scared us.

gl

1. _____

2. _____

4. _____

bl

1. _____

2. _____

3. _____

pl

1. _____

2. _____

3. _____

4. _____

🍎 **WRITE Write a sentence for each Core Word on a separate sheet of paper.**

MEANING STRATEGY Write the Core Words that best complete the letter. Use each word only once.

Dear Jake

_____

We _____ to have a picnic on the

_____

Fourth of July. I am very _____. Everyone on our

_____

_____ will come. We will bring a peach and a

_____   _____

_____ for a snack. There will be a _____ of punch for

_____

everyone. We will _____ apple and pear juice to make it.

_____

The fireworks show will be held on a big _____ of

_____

land. We will watch the fireworks _____ off. If you

_____

_____, you'll miss them!

_____

Fireworks _____ a picnic will add up to a good time for all.

Core Words

1. plus
2. glass
3. blink
4. plot
5. glad
6. blend
7. plan
8. block
9. plum
10. blast

Challenge Words

blank
blanket
planet
glue
gloves

VISUALIZATION STRATEGY Figure out the letters and write the Core Words.

1. ___ ___ ad

2. ___ ___ ast

3. ___ ___ us

4. ___ ___ end

5. ___ ___ an

6. ___ ___ ink

7. ___ ___ um

8. ___ ___ ock

9. ___ ___ ot

Add the underlined word parts together to make Challenge Words.

1. g<u>lee</u> + d<u>oves</u> = _____

2. <u>bl</u>ue + s<u>ank</u> = _____

3. <u>g</u>o + b<u>lue</u> = _____

4. <u>plan</u>t + n<u>et</u>s = _____

5. <u>blank</u> + s<u>et</u> = _____

PROOFREADING STRATEGY Here is a draft of one student's invitation to a picnic. Find three misspelled Core Words. Circle them and write them correctly.

Proofreading Marks	
⬭	misspelling
⊙	add a period
＝	make a capital letter

    Please plain to come to our picnic on the Fourth of July. I will be so glod. We will have food plas games.

1. _____

2. _____

3. _____

 MEANING STRATEGY Invitation
Plan to write an invitation to a friend for a Fourth of July picnic. Think about what you might like to say on your invitation. Choose and write at least three Core Words that you will use in your invitation. Write your story on a separate sheet of paper.

1. _____ 2. _____ 3. _____

Now proofread your word list and invitation and correct any errors.

11 Words with *sk*, *mp*, and *ng*

Core Words

1. wing
2. dump
3. sting
4. mask
5. long
6. jump
7. desk
8. song
9. camp
10. ask

My Words

Spelling Focus—The /sk/ sound can be spelled *sk*. The /mp/ sound can be spelled *mp*. The /ng/ sound can be spelled *ng*. *mp* and *ng* are never found at the beginning of words.

VISUALIZATION STRATEGY
Write the Core Words with the following spellings.

Core Word Sentences

The bird's **wing** is broken.
You'll find junk at the **dump**.
The angry bee will **sting**.
He drew eyes on the **mask**.
Do you **long** for your home?
He will **jump** into the air.
Sit at your own **desk**.
Let's sing a **song**.
Let's **camp** outside.
Can I **ask** you a question?

mp

1. _____
_____
2. _____
_____
3. _____

ng

1. _____
_____
2. _____
3. _____
4. _____

sk

1. _____
2. _____
3. _____

MEANING STRATEGY Write the Core Words that best complete the story. Use each word only once.

Camping Fun

Before you _____ in the woods, sit at your

_____ and write a list of things you must remember.

Be sure to _____ where to put your tent. Bugs

may _____, so bring a spray. Take a _____

walk every day. Look for a bird with red on its _____.

When you spot a raccoon, look for the _____ on its

face. Watch a frog _____ over a log. Sing a happy

camp _____ every evening. Finally, remember to

_____ your trash in a can before you leave.

Core Words

1. wing
2. dump
3. sting
4. mask
5. long
6. jump
7. desk
8. song
9. camp
10. ask

Challenge Words

blimp
grump
stamp
bring
task

VISUALIZATION STRATEGY Add *sk, mp,* or *ng* to write the Core Words.

a _ _
1. _____

de _ _
2. _____

ma _ _
3. _____

ca _ _
4. _____

du _ _
5. _____

ju _ _
6. _____

lo _ _
7. _____

so _ _
8. _____

sti _ _
9. _____

wi _ _
10. _____

PRONUNCIATION STRATEGY Say and write the Challenge Words. Circle the letters that spell the ending sound in each word.

1. _____

2. _____

3. _____

4. _____

5. _____

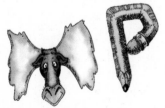

PROOFREADING STRATEGY Here is a draft of one student's rules about camp. Find four misspelled Core Words. Circle them and write them correctly.

Proofreading Marks
⬭ misspelling
⊙ add a period
═ make a capital letter

1. Do not junp on the bed.
2. Take your trash to the domp.
3. Write a log letter home every week.
4. Get help for a bee steng.

1. _____
2. _____
3. _____
4. _____

MEANING STRATEGY Rules
Plan to write some rules for going on a camping trip. Think of some good rules to have when you go camping. Choose and write at least three Core Words that you will use in your list of rules. Write your rules on a separate sheet of paper.

1. _____ 2. _____ 3. _____

Now proofread your word list and rules and correct any errors.

12 Review for Lessons 7-11

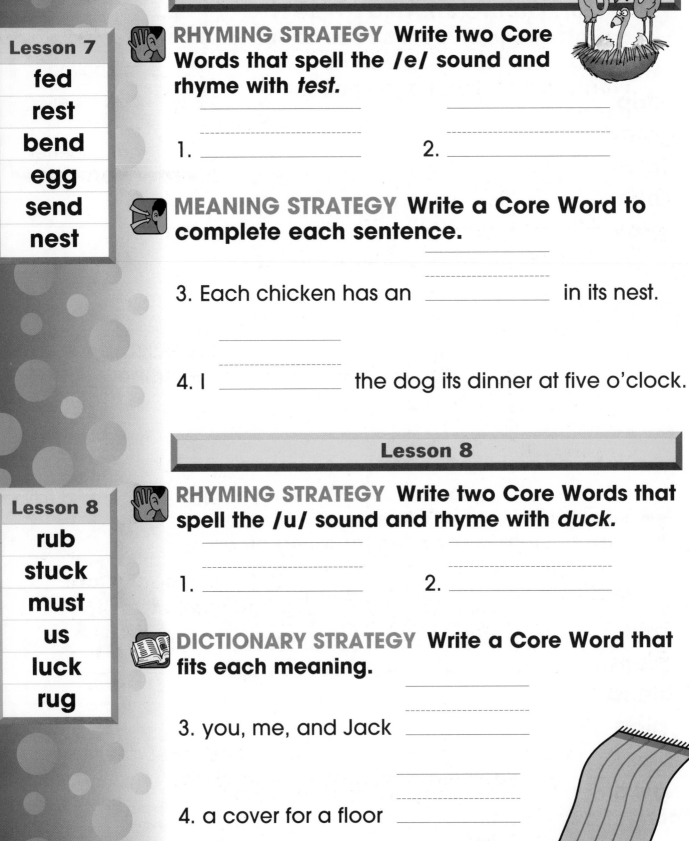

Lesson 7

Lesson 7
fed
rest
bend
egg
send
nest

RHYMING STRATEGY Write two Core Words that spell the /e/ sound and rhyme with *test*.

1. _____

2. _____

MEANING STRATEGY Write a Core Word to complete each sentence.

3. Each chicken has an _____ in its nest.

4. I _____ the dog its dinner at five o'clock.

Lesson 8

Lesson 8
rub
stuck
must
us
luck
rug

RHYMING STRATEGY Write two Core Words that spell the /u/ sound and rhyme with *duck*.

1. _____

2. _____

DICTIONARY STRATEGY Write a Core Word that fits each meaning.

3. you, me, and Jack _____

4. a cover for a floor _____

Review

Lesson 9

trip
drip
grand
truck
drum
gray

PRONUNCIATION STRATEGY Say each Core Word. Write two words that spell the /gr/ sound.

1. _____

2. _____

MEANING STRATEGY Write a Core Word that fits each group.

3. car, van, _____

4. fall, stumble, _____

PRONUNCIATION STRATEGY Say each Core Word. Write a word that has the same vowel sound.

5. him fill _____

6. tug duck _____

Lesson 10

Lesson 10

blink
plum
blend
plan
block
glad

PRONUNCIATION STRATEGY Say each Core Word. Write two words that spell the /pl/ sound.

1. _____

2. _____

CONVENTIONS STRATEGY Add one letter to each word to write a Core Word.

3. link _____

4. lock _____

Review

desk
camp
wing
dump
ask
song

💬 **PRONUNCIATION STRATEGY** Write two Core Words that spell the /sk/ sound.

1. _____   2. _____

🔤 **CONVENTIONS STRATEGY** Drop one or more letters from each word to write a Core Word.

3. camps _____   4. dumping _____

Spelling Strategy

THINK Look at the Core Word list on pages 48–50. Choose two words that are the hardest for you to spell. Write the words and a strategy to help you remember how to spell each word. For example: *Egg* is spelled with two *g*'s, one for the white and one for the yolk.

Words	Spelling Strategies
1.	
2.	

Review

 PROOFREADING STRATEGY Read the story. Find three misspelled Core Words. Circle them and write them correctly.

Proofreading Marks	
◯	misspelling
═	make a capital letter
⊙	add a period

It is not halloween yett. Halloween will come next Tuesday. I will be gladd then! I think october is a grend month because it has Halloween!

1. _____   2. _____   3. _____

Now find two words that should begin with a capital letter. Underline each letter three times to show it should be a capital letter.

 MEANING STRATEGY Article
Write an article for a school newspaper about a special event that took place at the school. Use at least four spelling words. First, write the spelling words that you want to use.

1. _____   3. _____

2. _____   4. _____

Now proofread your article and correct any errors.

Review

SPELLING FUN Use the following Core Words from Lessons 7–11 to complete the puzzle.

Lesson 7
rest
met
bend

Lesson 8
us
mud
rust
must

Lesson 9
grin
drive
grand

Lesson 10
plus
glass
blast

Lesson 11
sting
mask

ACROSS

3. Wet dirt
4. Smile
5. You and me
7. A bee does this.
9. Rhymes with *pet*
10. _____ off
11. It holds a drink.
12. Take a nap
13. We came to a _____ in the road.

DOWN

1. _____ a car
2. Rhymes with *dust*
3. Have to
6. Two _____ two is four.
8. We had a _____ time.
9. Worn on Halloween

Review

STANDARDIZED-FORMAT TEST PRACTICE

Choose the correct spelling of the Core Words from Lessons 7–11.

ANSWERS

SAMPLE	A. mudd	B. mude	C. mud	Ⓐ Ⓑ **Ⓒ**
1. A. drov	B. drofe	C. drove	Ⓐ Ⓑ Ⓒ
2. A. stuk	B. stuck	C. stuc	Ⓐ Ⓑ Ⓒ
3. A. gray	B. grae	C. gra	Ⓐ Ⓑ Ⓒ
4. A. saung	B. song	C. songe	Ⓐ Ⓑ Ⓒ

Choose the misspelled Core Words from Lessons 7–11.

SAMPLE	A. kamp	B. luck	C. drive	**Ⓐ** Ⓑ Ⓒ
1. A. tree	B. shutt	C. yet	Ⓐ Ⓑ Ⓒ
2. A. eg	B. tug	C. grin	Ⓐ Ⓑ Ⓒ
3. A. blast	B. plumm	C. rub	Ⓐ Ⓑ Ⓒ
4. A. jummp	B. test	C. plot	Ⓐ Ⓑ Ⓒ

Choose the correct spelling of the Core Words from Lessons 7–11 to complete each sentence.

SAMPLE	Did you _____ the door?			
	A. shet	B. shut	C. chut	Ⓐ **Ⓑ** Ⓒ

1. Two _____ two equals four.
   A. pluss   B. plus   C. plis   Ⓐ Ⓑ Ⓒ

2. He is wearing a _____.
   A. masc   B. massk   C. mask   Ⓐ Ⓑ Ⓒ

3. They _____ that way.
   A. went   B. wint   C. wend   Ⓐ Ⓑ Ⓒ

4. The snake was very _____.
   A. lang   B. lon   C. long   Ⓐ Ⓑ Ⓒ

13 The /ā/ Sound

Spelling Focus—The /ā/ sound can be spelled *ai*, *a_e*, or *ay*.

PRONUNCIATION STRATEGY Say each Core Word. Write the words with the /ā/ sound spelled the following ways. The *ay* spelling is often found at the end of words.

🍎 **Core Words**

1. came
2. bait
3. rake
4. hay
5. plate
6. pail
7. cane
8. raise
9. grape
10. say

My Words

Core Word Sentences

My wish **came** true!

The fish ate the **bait.**

I like to **rake** the leaves.

Horses eat **hay.**

Wipe the **plate** dry.

Fill the **pail** with sand.

Sugar comes from sugar **cane.**

Let's **raise** our hands high.

The **grape** had no seeds.

Please **say** what you want.

a_e

1. _____
2. _____
3. _____
4. _____
5. _____

ai

1. _____
2. _____
3. _____

ay

1. _____
2. _____

MEANING STRATEGY Write the Core Words that best complete the story. Use each word only once.

Gone Fishing

My friend and I like to fish. We made our own fishing rods

_____

from an old walking _____ and an old garden

_____

_____. The rake had been used to gather _____.

We use worms for _____. I would _____

that when we _____ the fishing line out of the water,

a fish is usually on the hook. One day we _____

home with ten fish in our _____. At supper, two fresh fish

were on each _____. They tasted great with some

vegetables, rice, and _____ juice.

Core Words

1. **came**
2. **bait**
3. **rake**
4. **hay**
5. **plate**
6. **pail**
7. **cane**
8. **raise**
9. **grape**
10. **say**

Challenge Words

aid

pain

trail

stain

blaze

RHYMING STRATEGY Write the Core Word that rhymes with each word.

1. mane _____

2. tape _____

3. make _____

4. fail _____

5. wait _____

6. play _____

7. haze _____

8. name _____

9. date _____

10. day _____

VISUALIZATION STRATEGY Write the Challenge Words hidden in these letters.

1. brsyaid _____

2. painkwlo _____

3. pntrailrs _____

4. jtusstain _____

5. blazecrdw _____

PROOFREADING STRATEGY Here is a draft of one student's newspaper story about fishing. Find four misspelled Core Words. Circle them and write them correctly.

Proofreading Marks

⬭	misspelling
⊙	add a period
=	make a capital letter

Yesterday two fish were caught off the town dock. Worms were used for bate. The fish were so big, they could not fit on a dinner plat. Many people kame to see them. Some sey they were the biggest fish they have ever seen!

1. _____

2. _____

3. _____

4. _____

MEANING STRATEGY Newspaper Story
Plan to write a newspaper story about fishing. Think about the things that can happen when people go fishing. Choose and write at least three Core Words that you will use in your newspaper story. Write your story on a separate sheet of paper.

1. _____ 2. _____ 3. _____

Now proofread your word list and newspaper story and correct any errors.

14 The /ē/ Sound

Spelling Focus—The /ē/ sound can be spelled *ea* or *ee*.

 VISUALIZATION STRATEGY Write the Core Words with the following spellings.

Core Word Sentences

Whales swim in **deep** water.
My favorite **meal** is dinner.
The **sheep** gives us wool.
He gave us **each** ten cents.
I'll **wheel** the baby stroller.
Ice cream is a real **treat.**
Jack planted the **bean.**
Have you **seen** my glasses?
Can I join the tennis **team?**
She woke from a **dream.**

🍎 **Core Words**

1. deep
2. meal
3. sheep
4. each
5. wheel
6. treat
7. bean
8. seen
9. team
10. dream

My Words

4. _____

5. _____

6. _____

ee

1. _____

2. _____

3. _____

4. _____

ea

1. _____

2. _____

3. _____

🍎 **WRITE Write a sentence for each Core Word on a separate sheet of paper.**

MEANING STRATEGY Write the Core Words that best complete the story. Use each word only once.

Sheep Team

I know a man who tends _____. He has a wagon

and two dogs that run beside the wagon's _____.

While the sheep graze, _____ dog circles the flock.

They work together as a _____. At noon, the man can

eat a _____ knowing that his flock is safe. Every

sheep will be _____ by the dogs. The man often eats

a dish made with a kind of _____. Then he falls into a

_____ sleep. At night, the dogs get a _____.

Then the dogs go to sleep and _____!

Core Words

1. deep
2. meal
3. sheep
4. each
5. wheel
6. treat
7. bean
8. seen
9. team
10. dream

Challenge Words

mean
leave
cream
sleep
sneeze

cr, sn, sl, l, m

eeze, ean, eep, eave, eam

VISUALIZATION STRATEGY Change one or more letters in each word and write a Core Word.

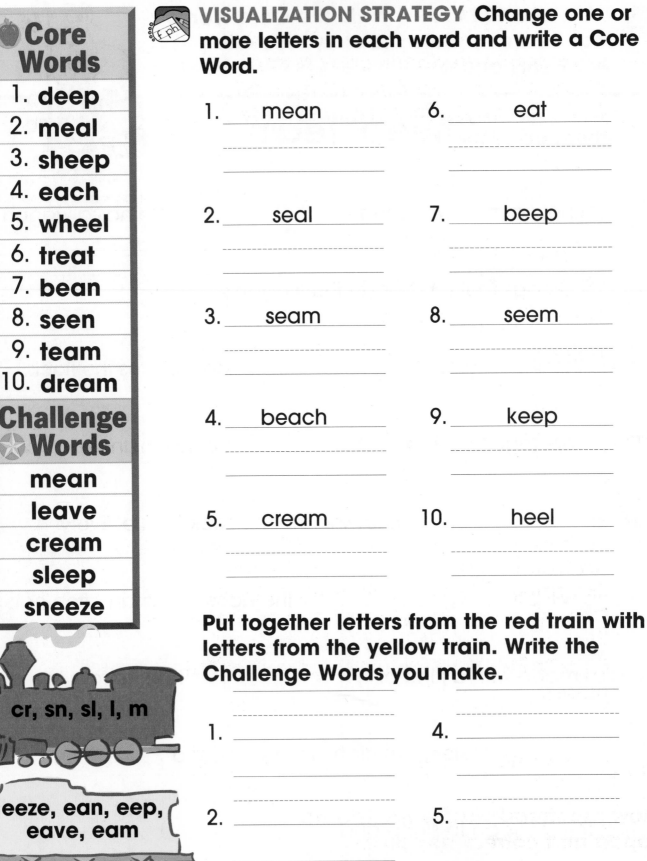

1. _____ mean _____

6. _____ eat _____

2. _____ seal _____

7. _____ beep _____

3. _____ seam _____

8. _____ seem _____

4. _____ beach _____

9. _____ keep _____

5. _____ cream _____

10. _____ heel _____

Put together letters from the red train with letters from the yellow train. Write the Challenge Words you make.

1. _____

4. _____

2. _____

5. _____

3. _____

PROOFREADING STRATEGY Here is a draft of one student's book report about sheep. Find three misspelled Core Words. Circle them and write them correctly.

Proofreading Marks

⬭	misspelling
⊙	add a period
=	make a capital letter

> My favorite book is about shep. They live on a big farm. I read some pages ech day. It helps me learn about animals and how to tret them.

1. _____

2. _____

3. _____

 MEANING STRATEGY Book Report
Plan to write a book report about your favorite book. Think about what you like about the book you have chosen. Choose and write at least three Core Words that you will use in your report. Write your report on a separate sheet of paper.

1. _____ 2. _____ 3. _____

Now proofread your word list and report and correct any errors.

15 The /ī/ Sound

Spelling Focus—The /ī/ sound can be spelled *y, i_e,* or *igh.*

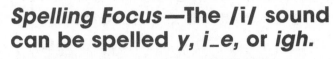 **VISUALIZATION STRATEGY** Write the Core Words with the following spellings.

🍎 Core Words

1. shy
2. right
3. wide
4. light
5. pine
6. fight
7. fly
8. night
9. dry
10. sight

My Words

Core Word Sentences

The **shy** student sat alone.

Do you turn left or **right?**

The window is **wide** open.

Please **light** the candles.

The **pine** tree grew tall.

Don't **fight** over the toy.

Birds **fly** high in the sky.

It is dark at **night.**

He will **dry** the wet dish.

A rainbow is a rare **sight.**

i_e

1. _____

2. _____

igh

1. _____

2. _____

3. _____

4. _____

5. _____

y

1. _____

2. _____

3. _____

🍎 **WRITE** Write a sentence for each Core Word on a separate sheet of paper.

MEANING STRATEGY Write the Core Words that best complete the story. Use each word only once.

Dear Tony

Do you want to go on a plane

ride with me? In the daytime, we will

_____

see many things because it is _____. We can

_____ _____

_____ over houses and a _____ forest. We

_____

will soar over the long, _____ river below us. At

_____

_____, we will see the city lights.

_____

We will not _____ over the window seat. Do not be

_____ _____

_____ about saying you are scared. Just _____

_____

your eyes. Look to both the left and _____. I know you

_____

will enjoy each wonderful _____!

VOWEL-SUBSTITUTION STRATEGY Add *i_e, y,* or *igh* to write the Core Words.

1. s ___ ___ ___ t

6. s h ___

2. p ___ n ___

7. f ___ ___ ___ t

3. n ___ ___ ___ t

8. w ___ d

4. d r ___

9. l ___ ___ ___ t

5. r ___ ___ ___ t

10. f l ___

PRONUNCIATION STRATEGY Say each Challenge Word. Write the words that rhyme with these words.

sight

1. _____

2. _____

shy

3. _____

4. _____

pipe

5. _____

PROOFREADING STRATEGY Here is a draft of one student's report about the weather. Find four misspelled Core Words. Circle them and write them correctly.

Proofreading Marks

⬭	misspelling
⊙	add a period
=	make a capital letter

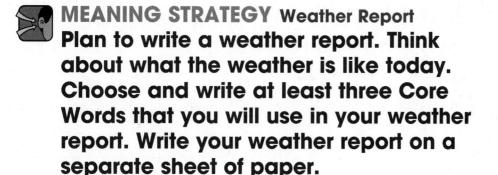

Today will be fair and dri. Clouds will move in at nit. It will rain rite after midnight. Pilots should not flie their planes. Stay at home until the sky clears!

1. _____

2. _____

3. _____

4. _____

 **MEANING STRATEGY** Weather Report
Plan to write a weather report. Think about what the weather is like today. Choose and write at least three Core Words that you will use in your weather report. Write your weather report on a separate sheet of paper.

1. _____   2. _____   3. _____

Now proofread your word list and weather report and correct any errors.

16 The /ō/ Sound

Spelling Focus—The /ō/ sound can be spelled oa, o_e, or ow.

Core Words

1. poke
2. boat
3. row
4. goat
5. snow
6. toad
7. soap
8. blow
9. coat
10. tow

My Words

VISUALIZATION STRATEGY Write the Core Words with the following spellings.

Core Word Sentences

He got a **poke** in the eye.

The **boat** sailed away.

Can you **row** a boat?

The **goat** kicked the can.

The **snow** is falling.

The **toad** lives in the pond.

Wash your hands with **soap.**

We can **blow** bubbles.

Please **coat** the pan with oil.

They will **tow** the car away.

4. _____

5. _____

o_e

1. _____

ow

1. _____

2. _____

3. _____

4. _____

oa

1. _____

2. _____

3. _____

WRITE Write a sentence for each Core Word on a separate sheet of paper.

MEANING STRATEGY Write the Core Words that best complete the story. Use each word only once.

Up in the Mountains

The mountain _____ leaps

from rock to rock like a _____ jumping

from log to log. It races over the hills like a _____ over

water. It would be as hard to catch as a wet bar of _____.

It is strong and could _____ a heavy load.

Ice and _____ often cover the rocks of its home.

Sometimes a cold wind will _____. The goat has a thick

_____ of fur. It has to _____ its nose around to

find food. It might find a _____ of plants on the hillside.

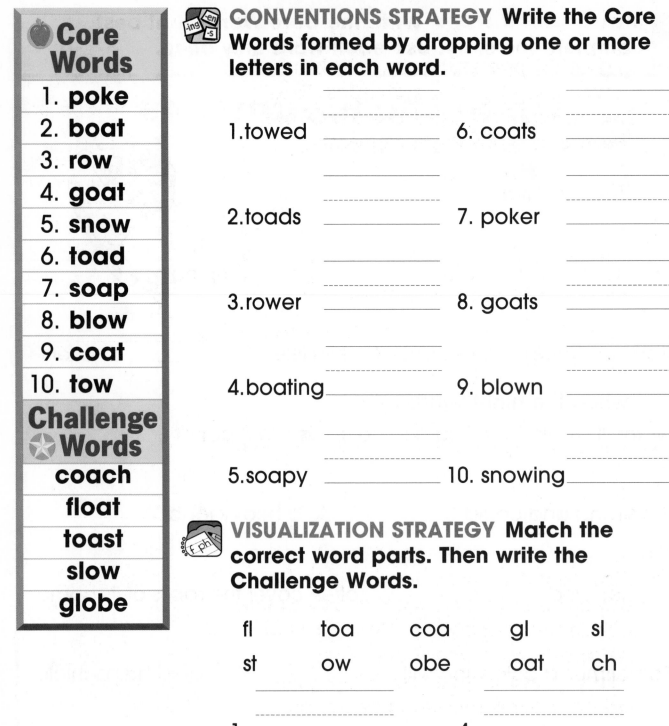

Core Words

1. poke
2. boat
3. row
4. goat
5. snow
6. toad
7. soap
8. blow
9. coat
10. tow

Challenge Words

coach
float
toast
slow
globe

CONVENTIONS STRATEGY Write the Core Words formed by dropping one or more letters in each word.

1. towed _____   6. coats _____

2. toads _____   7. poker _____

3. rower _____   8. goats _____

4. boating _____   9. blown _____

5. soapy _____   10. snowing _____

VISUALIZATION STRATEGY Match the correct word parts. Then write the Challenge Words.

| fl | toa | coa | gl | sl |
| st | ow | obe | oat | ch |

1. _____   4. _____

2. _____   5. _____

3. _____

PROOFREADING STRATEGY Here is a draft of one student's ad about summer and winter activities. Find four misspelled Core Words. Circle them and write them correctly.

Proofreading Marks

◯ misspelling

⊙ add a period

= make a capital letter

> In summer, roe a boat or go hiking. Perhaps you will see a mountain gote or a toad. In winter, play in the snoe. Then sit by the fire when the night winds bloo.

1. _____

2. _____

3. _____

4. _____

 MEANING STRATEGY Ad
Plan to write an ad for a trip to the mountains. Think about what you like about the mountains. Choose and write at least three Core Words that you will use in your ad. Write your ad on a separate sheet of paper.

1. _____   2. _____   3. _____

Now proofread your word list and ad and correct any errors.

17 The /oo/ Sound

Core Words

1. tune
2. moon
3. pool
4. zoo
5. rude
6. soon
7. boot
8. food
9. tube
10. room

My Words

_____

_____

_____

_____

Spelling Focus—The /oo/ sound can be spelled u_e or oo.

 VISUALIZATION STRATEGY
Write the Core Words with the following spellings.

Core Word Sentences

Can you sing that **tune?**

The **moon** rose in the sky.

We can **pool** our money.

We saw tigers at the **zoo.**

It is **rude** to be so late.

We will be home **soon.**

The **boot** fits over my shoe.

We bought **food** for dinner.

A **tube** fits inside a tire.

I will clean my **room.**

u_e

1. _____

2. _____

3. _____

oo

1. _____

2. _____

3. _____

4. _____

5. _____

6. _____

7. _____

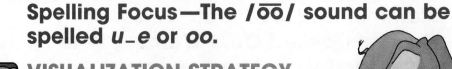 **WRITE Write a sentence for each Core Word on a separate sheet of paper.**

MEANING STRATEGY Write the Core Words that best complete the story. Use each word only once.

A Fun Place to Visit

Have you ever gone to the _____? You can watch

the seals swim in a _____. They have a lot of _____

to swim and dive. They have a slide that is a long, hollow

_____. Sometimes they will clap their flippers if someone

plays them a _____. The animal trainer gives them

_____. The seals share. They are not _____. If you

stay until night, you might see the _____. But you must

go home _____. If not, a zookeeper

might _____ you out!

Core Words

1. tune
2. moon
3. pool
4. zoo
5. rude
6. soon
7. boot
8. food
9. tube
10. room

Challenge Words

moose
goose
zoom
balloon
shoot

VOWEL-SUBSTITUTION STRATEGY Fill in the missing vowels to write the Core Words.

1. r ___ ___ m

2. b ___ ___ t

3. t ___ n

4. r ___ d

5. m ___ ___ n

6. s ___ ___ n

7. t ___ b ___

8. z ___ ___

9. f ___ ___ d

10. p ___ ___ l

VISUALIZATION STRATEGY Unscramble these letters to write the Challenge Words.

1. ozom _____

2. osoge _____

3. soemo _____

4. thoos _____

5. lonolab _____

PROOFREADING STRATEGY Here is a draft of one student's list of questions about working at a zoo. Find three misspelled Core Words. Circle them and write them correctly.

Proofreading Marks
⬭   misspelling
⊙   add a period
=   make a capital letter

1. Do you like working at the zu?
2. What fod do you feed the lions?
3. How often do you clean the seal poole?

1. _____

2. _____

3. _____

MEANING STRATEGY List of Questions Plan to write a list of questions you would like to ask a zookeeper. Think about what you would like to know about working in a zoo. Choose and write at least three Core Words that you will use in your list. Write your list of questions on a separate sheet of paper.

1. _____
2. _____
3. _____

Now proofread your word list and questions and correct any errors.

18 Review for Lessons 13-17

Lesson 13

hay
bait
say
grape
pail
cane

VISUALIZATION STRATEGY Write two Core Words that spell the /ā/ sound for the pattern *ay*.

1. _____   2. _____

MEANING STRATEGY Write a Core Word to complete each sentence.

3. Get the rod, then put _____ on the hook.

4. He has to walk with a _____.

5. Carry the water in a _____.

Lesson 14

Lesson 14

bean
meal
treat
dream
each
wheel

VISUALIZATION STRATEGY Write two Core Words that spell the /ē/ sound for the pattern *ea*.

1. _____   2. _____

RHYMING STRATEGY Write the Core Word that rhymes with each word.

3. seam _____   5. peach _____

4. heel _____   6. heat _____

Review

Lesson 15

shy

night

fly

right

pine

fight

VISUALIZATION STRATEGY Write two Core Words that spell the /ī/ sound for the pattern *y*.

1. _____   2. _____

MEANING STRATEGY Write a Core Word that means the opposite of each word.

3. wrong _____   4. day _____

CONVENTIONS STRATEGY Write the Core Words formed by dropping the end letter or letters.

5. fighter _____   6. pines _____

Lesson 16

Lesson 16

goat

tow

coat

toad

poke

snow

VISUALIZATION STRATEGY Write two Core Words that spell the /ō/ sound for the pattern *ow*.

1. _____   2. _____

Unscramble these letters to write the Core Words.

3. keop _____   5. taod _____

4. toga _____   6. atco _____

Review

Lesson 17

food
tune
tube
soon
pool
room

VISUALIZATION STRATEGY Write two Core Words each that spell the /$\overline{oo}$/ sound for these patterns.

u_e   oo

1. _____   3. _____

_____   _____

2. _____   4. _____

MEANING STRATEGY Write a Core Word that fits each group of words.

_____   _____

5. later, now, _____ 6. lunch, apple, _____

Spelling Strategy

THINK Look at the Core Word lists on pages 74–76. Choose two words that are the hardest for you to spell. Write the word and a strategy to help you remember how to spell each word. For example: Please serve the *meal* to *me* and *Al*.

Words   **Spelling Strategies**

1. _____   _____

_____   _____

_____   _____

2. _____   _____

Review

 PROOFREADING STRATEGY **Read the story. Find three misspelled Core Words. Circle them and write them correctly.**

Proofreading Marks	
⬭	misspelling
⚌	make a capital letter
⊙	add a period

All nite long the sno fell This morning the ground was covered. So my friends and I built a fort Then we had a snowball fite!

1. _____ 2. _____ 3. _____

Now find two places where a period should be added. Use the correct proofreading mark to show where each period should be added.

 MEANING STRATEGY Questions
Write a list of questions for an interview with a circus performer. Use at least four spelling words. First write the spelling words that you want to use.

1. _____ 3. _____

2. _____ 4. _____

Now proofread your word list and questions and correct any errors.

Review

SPELLING FUN Use the following Core Words from Lessons 13–17 to complete the puzzle.

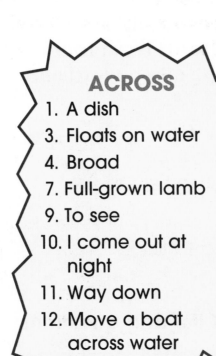

ACROSS
1. A dish
3. Floats on water
4. Broad
7. Full-grown lamb
9. To see
10. I come out at night
11. Way down
12. Move a boat across water

DOWN
2. Baseball group
3. _____ a bubble
5. When you sleep
6. Lift up
7. Used with water
8. Spins around
9. Type of flake

Review

Choose the correct spelling of the Core Words from Lessons 13–17.

ANSWERS

SAMPLE	A. raik	B. rayk	C. rake	Ⓐ Ⓑ **Ⓒ**
1.	A. came	B. kame	C. cam	Ⓐ Ⓑ Ⓒ
2.	A. pule	B. pul	C. pool	Ⓐ Ⓑ Ⓒ
3.	A. cain	B. cane	C. cayn	Ⓐ Ⓑ Ⓒ
4.	A. soap	B. sop	C. sope	Ⓐ Ⓑ Ⓒ

Choose the misspelled Core Words from Lessons 13–17.

SAMPLE	A. meel	B. coat	C. tune	**Ⓐ** Ⓑ Ⓒ
1.	A. seen	B. rake	C. zu	Ⓐ Ⓑ Ⓒ
2.	A. treet	B. dry	C. poke	Ⓐ Ⓑ Ⓒ
3.	A. grape	B. sheep	C. sigt	Ⓐ Ⓑ Ⓒ
4.	A. blow	B. right	C. bute	Ⓐ Ⓑ Ⓒ

Choose the correct spelling of the Core Words from Lessons 13–17 to complete each sentence.

SAMPLE They will arrive _____.		
A. soon B. soone C. sune	**Ⓐ** Ⓑ Ⓒ	

1. That man was very _____.
   A. rood   B. rud   C. rude   Ⓐ Ⓑ Ⓒ

2. The _____ was too bright.
   A. lite   B. light   C. ligt   Ⓐ Ⓑ Ⓒ

3. That _____ has a funny beard.
   A. goate   B. gote   C. goat   Ⓐ Ⓑ Ⓒ

4. The cow jumped over the_____.
   A. mun   B. moon   C. mune   Ⓐ Ⓑ Ⓒ

19 Words with *wh* and *sh*

Spelling Focus—The /hw/ sound can be spelled *wh*. The /sh/ sound can be spelled *sh*. *wh* is usually found at the beginning of a word.

PRONUNCIATION STRATEGY Say each Core Word. Write the words with the following spellings.

Core Words

1. what
2. clash
3. shock
4. while
5. shame
6. flash
7. where
8. shine
9. why
10. shore

My Words

Core Word Sentences

Did you hear **what** he said?

Do those colors **clash?**

The story may **shock** you.

Whistle **while** you work.

It is a **shame** you are sick.

We saw a **flash** of lightning.

This is **where** I live.

I gave my shoes a **shine.**

I know **why** the sky is blue.

The **shore** is rocky.

4. _____

begin with sh

1. _____

2. _____

3. _____

4. _____

begin with wh

1. _____

2. _____

3. _____

end with sh

1. _____

2. _____

MEANING STRATEGY Write the Core Words that best complete the story. Use each word only once.

Our School Band

Can you guess _____ I play the cymbals? I love to

make noise! Once we played on the _____ of a lake.

We hoped the sun would _____ all day. Do you know

_____ happened? We all got a sudden _____

as it grew dark. There was a bright _____ of light!

We did not know _____ it came from. Then a loud

_____ of thunder made us jump.

We could not play _____ it rained. It was a

_____ that we could not finish the concert.

Core Words

1. what
2. clash
3. shock
4. while
5. shame
6. flash
7. where
8. shine
9. why
10. shore

Challenge Words

shall
share
shadow
whisper
whiskers

CONSONANT-SUBSTITUTION STRATEGY
Add one letter to each word to write the Core Word.

1. cash _____   5. hat _____

2. same _____   6. here _____

3. sock _____   7. lash _____

4. sore _____   8. wile _____

VISUALIZATION STRATEGY Add *wh* or *sh* to write the Challenge Words.

1. __ __ iskers _____   4. __ __ are _____

2. __ __ isper _____   5. __ __ adow _____

3. __ __ all _____

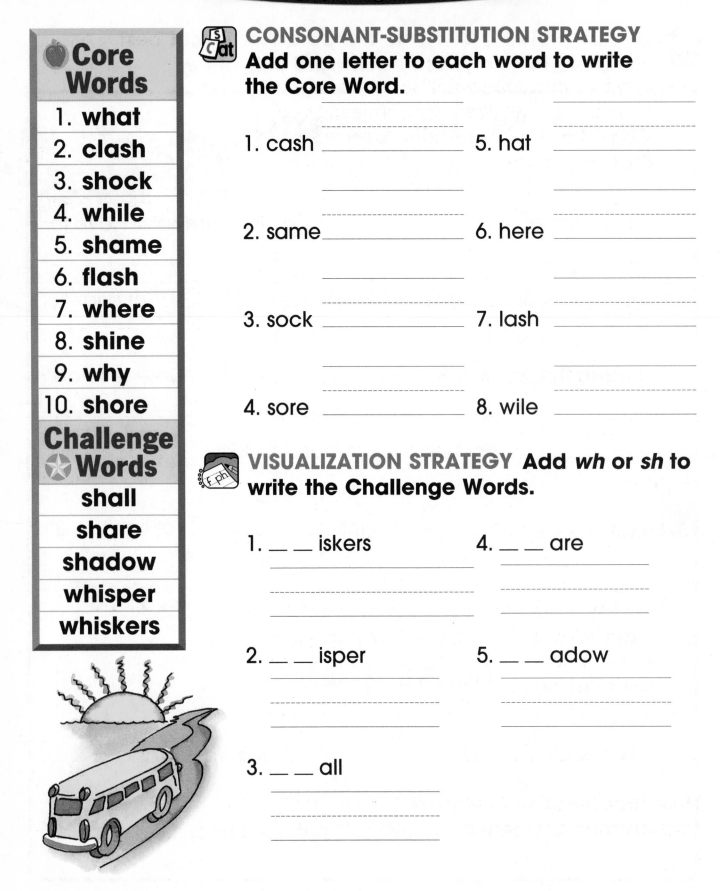

PROOFREADING STRATEGY Here is a draft of one student's song about moving away. Find three misspelled Core Words. Circle them and write them correctly.

Proofreading Marks
⬭ misspelling
⊙ add a period
= make a capital letter

> Oh, wy did you move?
> Oh, wher are you now?
> It is such a sham,
> Nothing is the same without you.

1. _____

2. _____

3. _____

 MEANING STRATEGY Song
Plan to write some new words to a song you like, such as a birthday song. Think of a song that goes well with the Core Words. Choose and write at least three Core Words that you will use in your song. Write your song on a separate sheet of paper.

1. _____   2. _____   3. _____

Now proofread your word list and song and correct any errors.

20 Words with *ch* and *th*

Spelling Focus—The /ch/ sound can be spelled *ch*. The /th/ sound can be spelled *th*.

Core Words

1. bath
2. peach
3. tooth
4. thin
5. choke
6. much
7. with
8. chick
9. teach
10. thank

My Words

PRONUNCIATION STRATEGY

Say each Core Word. Write the words with the following spellings.

Core Word Sentences

Fill the tub for your **bath.**

The **peach** has fuzzy skin.

A **tooth** of the comb broke.

My soup is **thin** and watery.

Don't **choke** on the candy.

How **much** do you have?

Please come **with** us.

The **chick** ate the worm.

Please **teach** me the trick.

I want to **thank** you.

begin with ch

1. _____

2. _____

end with th

1. _____

2. _____

3. _____

begin with th

1. _____

2. _____

end with ch

1. _____

2. _____

3. _____

 **WRITE** Write a sentence for each Core Word on a separate sheet of paper.

MEANING STRATEGY Write the Core Words that best complete the story. Use each word only once.

Growing Up

Yesterday I woke up _____ all of

my teeth in. But a _____ pit would change that.

I had so _____ to do. First, I had to feed the

hen's new _____ so it would not get too

_____. Then I wanted to _____ my dog

a new trick. Next, I gave my dog a _____. He did

not _____ me after I was done! At lunch, my

_____ fell out when I bit into a peach pit.

But I did not swallow my tooth and _____!

Core Words

1. bath
2. peach
3. tooth
4. thin
5. choke
6. much
7. with
8. chick
9. teach
10. thank

Challenge Words

child
chore
reach
thick
think

PRONUNCIATION STRATEGY Say each Core Word. Write the words that have the same vowel sound as these words.

sank bank

1. _____

give bit

2. _____

3. _____

4. _____

note wrote

5. _____

luck fun

6. _____

bead cream

7. _____

8. _____

bad can

9. _____

root tool

10. _____

VISUALIZATION STRATEGY Write the Challenge Words hidden in these letters.

1. srthickm _____

2. srthinkm _____

3. qdchildr _____

4. choremf _____

5. xgreach _____

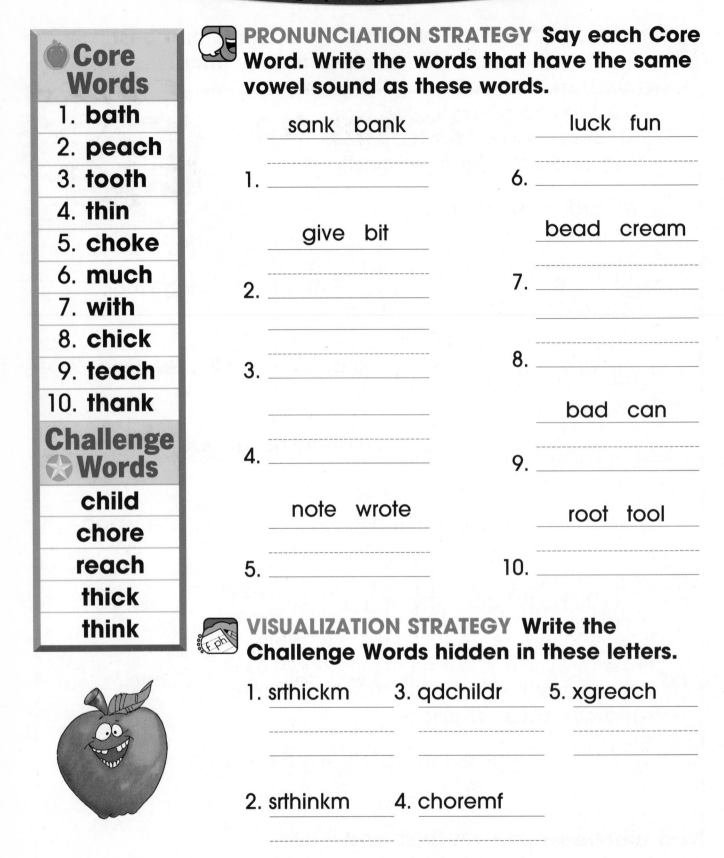

PROOFREADING STRATEGY Here is a draft of one student's diary entry about losing a tooth. Find four misspelled Core Words. Circle them and write them correctly.

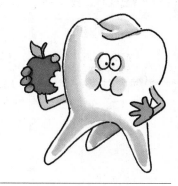

Proofreading Marks

⬭ misspelling

⊙ add a period

= make a capital letter

> Today I lost my front tuth. I was taking a bathe and playing whith my toys. Suddenly it fell out. It was a strange thig to happen.

1. _____

2. _____

3. _____

4. _____

 MEANING STRATEGY Diary Entry
Plan to write an entry in your diary about losing a tooth. Think about what it feels like to lose a tooth. Choose and write at least three Core Words that you will use in your diary entry. Write your entry on a separate sheet of paper.

1. _____   2. _____   3. _____

Now proofread your word list and diary entry and correct any errors.

21 The /är/ Sound

Spelling Focus—The /är/ sound can be spelled _ar_.

PRONUNCIATION STRATEGY Say each Core Word. Write the words with the following spellings.

Core Words

1. art
2. yard
3. barn
4. park
5. hard
6. cart
7. dark
8. farm
9. shark
10. sharp

My Words

_____

_____

_____

_____

_____

_____

_____

Core Word Sentences

The vase is a work of **art.**

Rake the leaves in the **yard.**

The cow is in the **barn.**

The swings are at the **park.**

A rock is very **hard.**

The pony pulled the **cart.**

The room is **dark.**

We cannot **farm** on this soil.

A **shark** has many teeth.

The pencil is **sharp.**

ard

1. _____

2. _____

arm

1. _____

arp

1. _____

arn

1. _____

art

1. _____

2. _____

ark

1. _____

2. _____

3. _____

WRITE Write a sentence for each Core Word on a separate sheet of paper.

MEANING STRATEGY Write the Core Words that best complete the story. Use each word only once.

Down on the Farm

My cousins live on a _____. Like most farmers, they

work _____. Just after sunrise, they fill a _____

with food for the pigs. Then they head for the _____

to milk the cows. Sometimes they work until it is _____.

On weekends, they cut the grass in the _____.

They keep the blades on the mower as _____ as

the teeth of a _____. For fun, they go to the

_____ to play ball. They also go to an _____

class. They always keep busy!

Core Words

1. **art**
2. **yard**
3. **barn**
4. **park**
5. **hard**
6. **cart**
7. **dark**
8. **farm**
9. **shark**
10. **sharp**

Challenge Words

harm

alarm

arms

march

smart

CONVENTIONS STRATEGY Write the Core Words formed by dropping one or more letters in each word.

1. part _____   6. sharks _____

2. farmer _____   7. sharper _____

3. hardy _____   8. carting _____

4. darkly _____   9. barns _____

5. spark _____   10. yards _____

VISUALIZATION STRATEGY Unscramble these letters to write the Challenge Words.

1. marla _____   4. tmars _____

2. marh _____   5. smar _____

3. harmc _____

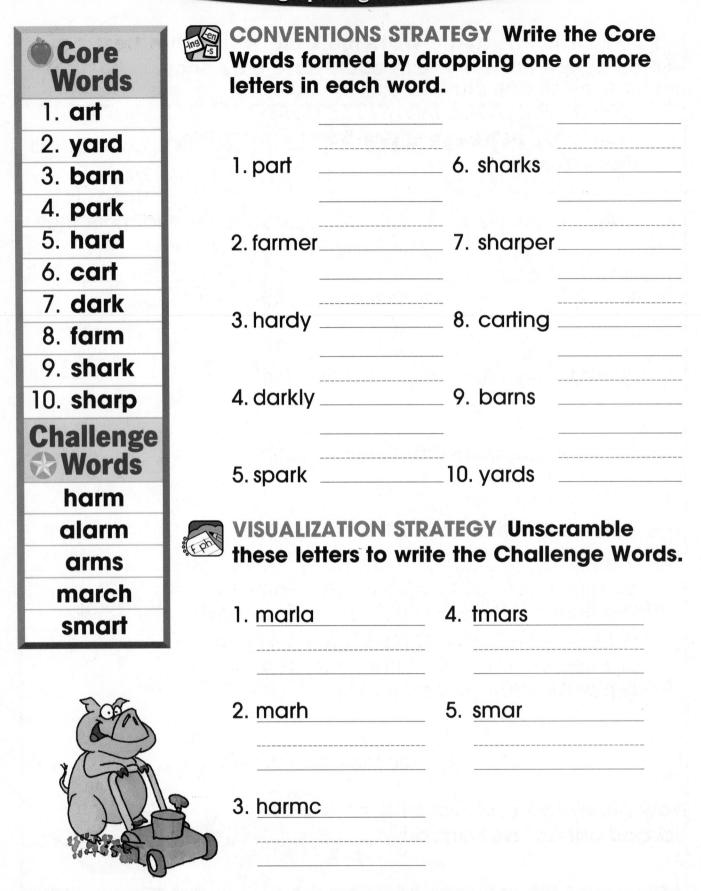

PROOFREADING STRATEGY Here is a draft of one student's list of farm chores. Find three misspelled Core Words. Circle them and write them correctly.

Proofreading Marks	
⬭	misspelling
⊙	add a period
=	make a capital letter

Farm Chores
1. Clean the born.
2. Fill the carte with hay.
3. Rake the yerd.
4. Feed the cows.

1. _____

2. _____

3. _____

 MEANING STRATEGY List of Chores
Plan to write a list of a farmer's chores during a normal day on a farm. Think of the things a farmer must do. Choose and write at least three Core Words that you will use on your list. Write your list on a separate sheet of paper.

1. _____ 2. _____ 3. _____

Now proofread your word list and chore list and correct any errors.

22 The /ûr/ and /or/ Sounds

Spelling Focus—The /ûr/ sound can be spelled ir. The /or/ sound can be spelled or.

Core Words

1. bird
2. more
3. shirt
4. horse
5. first
6. for
7. girl
8. horn
9. dirt
10. short

My Words

PRONUNCIATION STRATEGY Say each Core Word. Write the words with the following spellings.

Core Word Sentences

The **bird** flew away.

May I have **more** pie?

My **shirt** has three buttons.

Put a saddle on the **horse.**

She was the **first** in line.

Are you **for** or against my idea?

The **girl** invited the boy.

The cow had only one **horn.**

There is **dirt** on the floor.

The ladder is too **short.**

or

1. _____
2. _____
3. _____
4. _____
5. _____

ir

1. _____
2. _____
3. _____
4. _____
5. _____

WRITE Write a sentence for each Core Word on a separate sheet of paper.

MEANING STRATEGY Write the Core Words that best complete the story. Use each word only once.

Early One Morning

Sarah woke up very early when she heard a car

_____. The young _____ got out of bed quickly.

She put on pants and a _____. She wanted to enjoy her

_____ day of summer vacation.

A small brown _____ greeted her with a song. She

headed _____ the barn. It was only a _____ walk.

Inside, her _____ dug his hoof

in the _____ when he saw her. She

gave him some _____ hay to eat. Then she went riding.

Core Words

1. bird
2. more
3. shirt
4. horse
5. first
6. for
7. girl
8. horn
9. dirt
10. short

Challenge Words

store
morning
dinosaur
third
whirl

VISUALIZATION STRATEGY Take away one word by crossing out the letters. Write the Core Word that is left.

1. tshaolrlt – tall = _____

2. fliarsstt – last = _____

3. cdlieratn – clean = _____

4. gbioryl – boy = _____

5. briorbdin – robin = _____

6. sdhriersts – dress = _____

7. fforrom – from = _____

8. mloerses – less = _____

Add the underlined word parts together to write the Challenge Words.

1. <u>wh</u>at + <u>girl</u> = _____

2. <u>st</u>orm + a<u>re</u> = _____

3. <u>d</u>ie + <u>no</u>se + <u>au</u>to + a<u>re</u> = _____

4. <u>thi</u>n + <u>bird</u> = _____

5. <u>more</u> + <u>lin</u>ing = _____

PROOFREADING STRATEGY Here is a draft of a plan for morning activities. Find five misspelled Core Words. Circle them and write them correctly.

8:00–9:00	Make breakfast fer my family.
9:00–10:00	Buy a new red shert.
10:00–11:00	Go for a ride on my hors.
11:00–noon	Feed the berd one mor time.

Proofreading Marks

◯ misspelling

⊙ add a period

= make a capital letter

1. _____

2. _____

3. _____

4. _____

5. _____

MEANING STRATEGY Activity Plan
Write a plan about your activities for a summer morning. Think about what you would do on a beautiful summer morning. Choose and write at least three Core Words that you will use in your plan. Write your plan on a separate sheet of paper.

1. _____ 2. _____ 3. _____

Now proofread your word list and plan and correct any errors.

23 Easily Misspelled Words

Spelling Focus—Some words are not spelled as they sound. You must remember the letters that spell these words.

PRONUNCIATION STRATEGY Say each Core Word. Write the words that fit into the following categories.

Core Words

1. does
2. were
3. every
4. very
5. give
6. live
7. thing
8. your
9. many
10. who

My Words

Core Word Sentences

How **does** the clock work?

They **were** gone an hour.

We went on **every** ride.

She woke up **very** late.

Do not **give** me the book.

Frogs **live** on insects.

He has one **thing** to do.

I will visit **your** house.

Did **many** come to visit?

Guess **who** came.

one syllable

1. _____

_____

2. _____

_____

3. _____

_____

4. _____

_____

5. _____

_____

6. _____

7. _____

two syllables

1. _____

_____

2. _____

_____

3. _____

WRITE Write a sentence for each Core Word on a separate sheet of paper.

MEANING STRATEGY Write the Core Words that best complete the story. Use each word only once.

Road Race

Is there someone you know _____ likes to run?

Maybe it is someone in _____ family. Maybe it's you!

It _____ not matter where you _____. You can

find a place to run _____ day.

There are probably _____ races near where you

live. Some races are _____ long. Running in long races

is a hard _____ to do. The runners have to _____

their best. How would you

feel if you _____ in a long race?

Core Words

1. does
2. were
3. every
4. very
5. give
6. live
7. thing
8. your
9. many
10. who

Challenge Words

any
away
goes
find
kind

 VISUALIZATION STRATEGY Write the Core Words hidden in these letters.

1. jnevery _____

2. sthingl _____

3. lvmany _____

4. szwere _____

5. yourkw _____

6. lxwhop _____

7. doesci _____

8. ovvery _____

9. liveyh _____

10. givetu _____

 VOWEL-SUBSTITUTION STRATEGY Fill in the missing vowels to write the Challenge Words. Remember that the letter *y* is sometimes used as a vowel.

1. k _ n d _____

2. f _ n d _____

3. _ n _ _____

4. _ w _ _ _____

5. g _ _ s _____

PROOFREADING STRATEGY Here is a draft of a student's postcard about a race. Find three misspelled Core Words. Circle them and write them correctly.

Proofreading Marks
⬭ misspelling
⊙ add a period
＝ make a capital letter

Dear Alice,

I am vary happy you won the race. Did they giv you a medal? Will you run in any races? Hu came in second?

Nick

1. _____

2. _____

3. _____

 MEANING STRATEGY Postcard
Plan to write a postcard to a friend who has just won a race. Think about what you would like to say to your friend. Choose and write at least three Core Words that you will use in your postcard. Write your postcard on a separate sheet of paper.

1. _____ 2. _____ 3. _____

Now proofread your word list and postcard and correct any errors.

Lesson 19

Lesson 19
while
shore
shine
flash
shame
shock

PRONUNCIATION STRATEGY Say each Core Word. Write two words that spell the /sh/ sounds.

1. _____   2. _____

Write the words that have the same vowel sounds as these words.

3. lot, top, _____   5. store, for, _____

4. pile, mile, _____   6. dash, hat, _____

Lesson 20

Lesson 20
chick
bath
teach
thank
thin
choke

PRONUNCIATION STRATEGY Say each Core Word. Write two words that spell the /th/ sound.

1. _____   2. _____

MEANING STRATEGY Write a Core Word to complete each sentence. The missing word will rhyme with the underlined word.

3. Ben has to <u>pick</u> a _____ on the farm.

4. He will need a _____ <u>pin</u> to sew small things.

Review

Lesson 21
shark
farm
yard
barn
dark
hard

RHYMING STRATEGY Say each Core Word. Write two words that spell the /är/ sound for the pattern *ard.*

1. _____   2. _____

MEANING STRATEGY Write a Core Word that fits each group of words.

3. farm, tractor, _____

4. seal, tuna, _____

VISUALIZATION STRATEGY Write the Core Words hidden in these letters.

5. farmbku _____

6. nldarkdw _____

Lesson 22
shirt
bird
horn
short
girl
for

VISUALIZATION STRATEGY Write two Core Words that spell the /ûr/ sound for the pattern *ir.*

1. _____   2. _____

CONVENTIONS STRATEGY Write the Core Words that are formed by dropping one or more letters in each word.

3. fore _____

4. horned _____

Review

Lesson 23

live
were
who
does
give
very

 PRONUNCIATION STRATEGY Say each Core Word. Write two words that are one syllable and not spelled the way they sound.

1. _____   2. _____

VISUALIZATION STRATEGY Do these word problems. Then write the Core Word.

3. wed – d + re =   4. lift – ft + ve =

_____   _____

Spelling Strategy

THINK Look at the Core Word lists on pages 100–102. Choose two words that are the hardest for you to spell. Write the word and a strategy to help you remember how to spell each word. For example: *Your* house and *our* house are spelled alike.

Words	Spelling Strategies
1. _____	_____
2. _____	_____

Review

 PROOFREADING STRATEGY Read the story. Find three misspelled Core Words. Circle them and write them correctly.

Proofreading Marks	
⬭	misspelling
⹀	make a capital letter
⊙	add a period

acting is an artt. an actor can teech us about shaim or love or shock. Acting is hard to do. Do you like to act?

1. _____ 2. _____ 3. _____

Now find two words that should begin with a capital letter. Underline each letter three times to show it should be a capital letter.

MEANING STRATEGY Story
Write a funny story about discovering life on another planet. Use at least four spelling words. First, write the spelling words that you want to use.

1. _____ 3. _____

2. _____ 4. _____

Now proofread your story and correct any errors.

Review

🍎 **SPELLING FUN** Use the following Core Words from Lessons 19–23 to complete this puzzle.

Lesson 19
where
shame

Lesson 20
with

Lesson 21
park
hard
cart
sharp
art

Lesson 22
dirt

Lesson 23
does
were
every
thing
your
give

ACROSS

1. What is in your garden
4. All
6. Please_____ it to me.
8. Not soft but _____
10. A sorry feeling
11. A grocery _____
12. A green place for fun
14. Come_____ me.

DOWN

2. Rhymes with *ring*
3. We _____ not ready.
5. Is this _____ hat?
7. Question word about a place
9. I do; he _____.
10. The knife has a _____ point.
13. Crayons and paint are tools for this.

Review

STANDARDIZED-FORMAT TEST PRACTICE

🍎 **Choose the correct spelling of the Core Words from Lessons 19–23.**

ANSWERS

SAMPLE	A. whith	B. with	C. withe	Ⓐ **Ⓑ** Ⓒ
1. A. klash	B. clash	C. clach	Ⓐ Ⓑ Ⓒ
2. A. hors	B. horce	C. horse	Ⓐ Ⓑ Ⓒ
3. A. peach	B. peech	C. peich	Ⓐ Ⓑ Ⓒ
4. A. kart	B. cart	C. carrt	Ⓐ Ⓑ Ⓒ

🍎 **Choose the misspelled Core Words from Lessons 19–23.**

SAMPLE	A. sharp	B. durt	C. where	Ⓐ **Ⓑ** Ⓒ
1. A. what	B. liv	C. barn	Ⓐ Ⓑ Ⓒ
2. A. farem	B. shine	C. much	Ⓐ Ⓑ Ⓒ
3. A. more	B. why	C. hoo	Ⓐ Ⓑ Ⓒ
4. A. teech	B. dark	C. many	Ⓐ Ⓑ Ⓒ

🍎 **Choose the correct spelling of the Core Words from Lessons 19–23 to complete each sentence.**

SAMPLE	You gave me quite a _____.			
	A. shok	B. shak	C. shock	Ⓐ Ⓑ **Ⓒ**

1. Jane lost a _____.
   A. toothe   B. tuth   C. tooth   Ⓐ Ⓑ Ⓒ

2. He came in _____ place.
   A. ferst   B. first   C. furst   Ⓐ Ⓑ Ⓒ

3. _____ bus is full of students.
   A. Evry   B. Evrey   C. Every   Ⓐ Ⓑ Ⓒ

4. That _____ is in my class.
   A. girl   B. gerl   C. gurl   Ⓐ Ⓑ Ⓒ

25 Words with *br*, *fr*, and *tr*

Spelling Focus—The /tr/ sound can be spelled *tr*. The /br/ sound can be spelled *br*. The /fr/ sound can be spelled *fr*.

PRONUNCIATION STRATEGY Say each Core Word. Write the words with the following spellings.

Core Words

1. brag
2. trade
3. brick
4. frisky
5. train
6. frog
7. trick
8. broom
9. free
10. bright

My Words

Core Word Sentences

She will **brag** about herself.
Let's **trade** baseball cards!
Our house is made of **brick.**
The **frisky** dog leaped.
The **train** arrived late.
A **frog** croaked loudly.
The **trick** fooled everyone.
Sweep with the **broom.**
You are **free** to go.
The sun is **bright.**

br

1. _____

2. _____

3. _____

4. _____

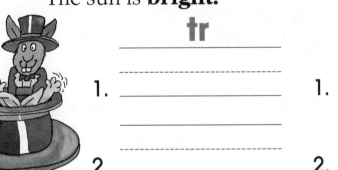

tr

1. _____

2. _____

3. _____

fr

1. _____

2. _____

3. _____

WRITE Write a sentence for each Core Word on a separate sheet of paper.

MEANING STRATEGY Write the Core Words that best complete the story. Use each word only once.

My Pet and I

I have a pet _____. It is _____

green. I found it in a pond. So I got it for _____ !

I try not to _____ too much about my pet. It is very

smart and very _____. I plan to _____ my

frog to do tricks. One _____ it has already learned is

jumping through a hoop.

My friend also has a pet frog. Sometimes we race our frogs on

the red _____ path in front of my house. We use the

handle of a _____ for the finish line.

I would not _____ my frog for any other pet.

Core Words

1. brag
2. trade
3. brick
4. frisky
5 train
6. frog
7. trick
8. broom
9. free
10. bright

Challenge Words

front
friend
bread
tramp
trace

VISUALIZATION STRATEGY Use these puzzle parts to make Core Words. Some parts will be used more than once.

oom   ee   fr   tr   br

ade   ain   og   ick   ag

1. _____   5. _____

2. _____   6. _____

3. _____   7. _____

4. _____   8. _____

Add *br*, *fr*, or *tr* to write the Challenge Words.

1. ____ ____iend   4. ____ ____ amp

2. ____ ____ace   5. ____ ____ead

3. ____ ____ ont

PROOFREADING STRATEGY Here is a draft of one student's story about a pet frog. Find three misspelled Core Words. Circle them and write them correctly.

Proofreading Marks	
⬭	misspelling
⊙	add a period
=	make a capital letter

> I have a new pet frog. It is brite green. I found it when I went fishing last week. It is very friske. It would be fun to train it to do a treck.

1. _____

2. _____

3. _____

 MEANING STRATEGY Story
Plan to write a story about a pet. Think about the kind of pet you have or would like to have. Choose and write at least three Core Words that you will use in your story. Write your story on a separate sheet of paper.

1. _____ 2. _____ 3. _____

Now proofread your word list and story and correct any errors.

26 Words with *sl* and *sp*

Spelling Focus—The /sl/ sound can be spelled *sl*. The /sp/ sound can be spelled *sp*.

PRONUNCIATION STRATEGY
Say each Core Word. Write the words with the following spellings.

Core Words

1. slam
2. speed
3. slip
4. spin
5. sled
6. space
7. slide
8. speech
9. slick
10. spy

My Words

Core Word Sentences

Don't **slam** the door.
Don't pass the **speed** limit.
He could **slip** on the ice.
Did the wheel **spin?**
I rode a **sled** down the hill.
Fill in the **space** with color.
I love the **slide** at the park.
We heard a short **speech.**
The wet road was **slick.**
The **spy** hid in the closet.

sl

1. _____

2. _____

3. _____

sp

1. _____

2. _____

3. _____

4. _____

5. _____

4. _____

5. _____

WRITE Write a sentence for each Core Word on a separate sheet of paper.

MEANING STRATEGY Write the Core Words that best complete the story. Use each word only once.

Fun in the Winter

I love the winter. When it snows, I pull my _____ to

the top of a hill, then I _____ down. I pick up

_____ going downhill. It feels as if I am flying

through _____. I have to be careful. I do not want to

_____ into a tree. At school, we heard

a _____ about winter safety.

I often go ice-skating on ice that is smooth

and _____. Sometimes I _____ and fall.

Other times I _____ like a top! Then I hope my friends

will _____ on me to see how well I skate!

Core Words

1. **slam**
2. **speed**
3. **slip**
4. **spin**
5. **sled**
6. **space**
7. **slide**
8. **speech**
9. **slick**
10. **spy**

Challenge Words

spoon

spoke

spark

sleet

slant

CONSONANT-SUBSTITUTION STRATEGY

Change one or two letters in each word to write a Core Word.

1. trace _____

2. greed _____

3. grin _____

4. sly _____

5. gram _____

6. fled _____

7. stick _____

8. glide _____

PRONUNCIATION STRATEGY

Say the name of each picture. Write the Challenge Words that begin like the picture name.

1. _____

2. _____

1. _____

2. _____

3. _____

PROOFREADING STRATEGY Here is a draft of one student's poem about ice-skating. Find three misspelled Core Words. Circle them and write them correctly.

> Ice-Skating
> I slep and slied,
> I just cannot glide.
> Please give me more spase,
> So I do not fall on my face!

Proofreading Marks

⬯ misspelling

⊙ add a period

= make a capital letter

1. _____

2. _____

3. _____

 MEANING STRATEGY Poem
Plan to write a poem about something you like to do in the winter. Think about a title for your poem. Choose and write at least three Core Words that you will use in your poem. Write your poem on a separate sheet of paper.

1. _____   2. _____   3. _____

Now proofread your word list and poem and correct any errors.

27 Words with -s

Spelling Focus—The letter *s* can be added to many words to make them mean "more than one." Words that name more than one are called *plurals*.

PRONUNCIATION STRATEGY Say each Core Word. Write the plural words that fit into each category.

Core Words

1. animals
2. ants
3. chickens
4. seals
5. cows
6. ducks
7. rabbits
8. snakes
9. whales
10. zebras

My Words

_____
_____
_____
_____

Core Word Sentences

The zoo has many **animals.**
I saw the **ants** crawl away.
The **chickens** laid the eggs.
He **seals** the envelope.
A farmer milked the **cows.**
The **ducks** are in the pond.
Two **rabbits** ate carrots.
Are you afraid of **snakes?**
Those **whales** are large.
The **zebras** have stripes.

one syllable

1. _____
2. _____
3. _____
4. _____
5. _____
6. _____

two syllables

1. _____
2. _____
3. _____

three syllables

1. _____

WRITE Write a sentence for each Core Word on a separate sheet of paper.

MEANING STRATEGY Write the Core Words that best complete the story. Use each word only once.

At the Zoo

A zoo has many kinds of _____. You may

hear _____ clucking and _____

quacking. You can watch _____ being milked and

feed furry _____. Bring a picnic lunch, but be

ready to share it with lots of black _____. After lunch,

you can visit the black and white _____. In the

reptile house, there are lizards and _____. You will

see harbor _____ in a pool. But you will not see any

blue _____. They are too big!

Core Words

1. **animals**
2. **ants**
3. **chickens**
4. **seals**
5. **cows**
6. **ducks**
7. **rabbits**
8. **snakes**
9. **whales**
10. **zebras**

Challenge Words

bears
lions
tigers
chipmunks
kangaroos

CONVENTIONS STRATEGY Adding *-s* to many nouns makes them plural. Make these words plural to match the Core Words.

1. ant _____

2. chicken _____

3. cow _____

4. duck _____

5. rabbit _____

6. snake _____

7. zebra _____

8. animal _____

9. seal _____

10. whale _____

PRONUNCIATION STRATEGY Say each Challenge Word. Write the words with the same vowel sounds as these words.

1. tear   wear _____

2. fine   like _____

3. sang   thank _____

4. this   stick _____

116   Words with *-s*

PROOFREADING STRATEGY Here is a draft of one student's report about whales. Find three misspelled Core Words. Circle them and write them correctly.

Proofreading Marks
⬭ misspelling
⊙ add a period
= make a capital letter

The biggest anmals in the world are wales. They live in the ocean just as seels do. They have flippers and fins. There are many kinds of whales. Some eat fish.

1. _____

2. _____

3. _____

 MEANING STRATEGY Report
Plan to write a report about an animal. Think about where your animal lives, what it eats, and how it looks. Choose and write at least three Core Words that you will use in your report. Write your report on a separate sheet of paper.

1. _____ 2. _____ 3. _____

Now proofread your word list and report and correct any errors.

28 Words That Sound Alike

Spelling Focus—Some words sound the same, but have different spellings and meanings. These words are called *homophones*.

PRONUNCIATION STRATEGY **Say each Core Word. Write the word pairs that sound the same.**

Core Words

1. see
2. road
3. meet
4. deer
5. die
6. meat
7. sea
8. dear
9. dye
10. rode

My Words

Core Word Sentences

I **see** better with glasses.

We drove on a winding **road.**

The track **meet** was great!

The **deer** lives in the woods.

Leaves **die** in the winter.

I eat fish but not **meat.**

Fish live in the **sea.**

She is a **dear** friend.

Did you **dye** the hat green?

We **rode** horses every day.

2. _____

3. _____

4. _____

1. _____

5. _____

DANGEROUS CURVES AHEAD!

WRITE **Write a sentence for each Core Word on a separate sheet of paper.**

MEANING STRATEGY Write the Core Words that best complete the story. Use each word only once.

A Bus Trip

Last year I visited my _____

cousin. I _____ on the bus. I saw a _____

by the _____. It ran right in front of the bus. Luckily,

we did not hit it. I am glad it did not get hurt and

_____. Later the bus stopped by the _____,

so we could _____ the sunset. The sky looked as if it

had been tinted with red _____.

My cousin was at the station to _____ me. That

night we ate a big meal of _____ and potatoes!

Core Words

1. see
2. road
3. meet
4. deer
5. die
6. meat
7. sea
8. dear
9. dye
10. rode

Challenge Words

seam

seem

eye

too

to

RHYMING STRATEGY Write the Core Words that rhyme with these words.

1. toad _____ _____

2. clear _____ _____

3. seat _____ _____

4. lie _____ _____

5. free _____ _____

VISUALIZATION STRATEGY Add the underlined word parts to write the Challenge Words.

1. t̲ip + d̲o̲ _____

2. t̲an + z̲o̲o̲ _____

3. s̲e̲e̲p + r̲a̲m̲ _____

4. s̲ad + b̲e̲a̲m̲ _____

5. e̲g̲g̲ + dr̲y̲ + b̲ak̲e̲ _____

PROOFREADING STRATEGY Here is a draft of one student's letter about a trip. Find four misspelled Core Words. Circle them and write them correctly.

Proofreading Marks
⬭ misspelling
⊙ add a period
═ make a capital letter

Dear Anita,

I went to sea my deer friend Jess. I drove on a bumpy rode. It was a real treat to meat her family.

Your friend,
Marty

1. _____

2. _____

3. _____

4. _____

 MEANING STRATEGY Letter
Plan to write a letter to a friend about a trip you have taken. Think about where you went and how you got there. Choose and write at least three Core Words that you will use in your letter. Write your letter on a separate sheet of paper.

1. _____ 2. _____ 3. _____

Now proofread your word list and letter and correct any errors.

29 Family Words

Spelling Focus—Some words tell about your family.

 VISUALIZATION STRATEGY Write the Core Words that end with the following letters.

Core Words

1. mother
2. family
3. grandfather
4. aunt
5. brother
6. grandmother
7. baby
8. sister
9. uncle
10. father

My Words

Core Word Sentences

My **mother** said we can go.

Her **family** lives there.

My **grandfather** is old.

My mom's sister is my **aunt.**

I have an older **brother.**

My **grandmother** sings.

The **baby** sleeps in the crib.

Share with your **sister.**

My **uncle** gave me a dollar.

His **father** drove us.

er

1. _____

2. _____

3. _____

4. _____

5. _____

6. _____

y

1. _____

2. _____

t

1. _____

le

1. _____

🍎 **WRITE** Write a sentence for each Core Word on a separate sheet of paper.

MEANING STRATEGY Write the Core Words that best complete the story. Use each word only once.

All in the Family

I have a large _____. We like to get together for

birthdays and holidays. Mom is the name I call my

_____. I call my _____ Dad. There is also a

little _____ who is two months old, a _____

named Jim, and a _____ named Fay. My mother's

sister is my _____. My mother's mother is my

_____. My father's brother is my

_____. My father's father is my

_____. And that's my family!

Core Words

1. mother
2. family
3. grandfather
4. aunt
5. brother
6. grandmother
7. baby
8. sister
9. uncle
10. father

Challenge Words

parent

person

twins

children

together

VISUALIZATION STRATEGY Fill in the missing letters to write the Core Words.

1. f _____ th _____ _____

2. m _____ th _____ _____

3. _____ _____ c _____ _____

4. s _____ s _____

5. b _____ _____ t _____ _____

6. f _____ m _____ _____ _____

7. b _____ b _____

Write the Challenge Words with these words in them.

1. get _____

2. child _____

3. son _____

4. rent _____

5. wins _____

PROOFREADING STRATEGY Here is a draft of one student's paragraph about a special aunt. Find four misspelled Core Words. Circle them and write them correctly.

Proofreading Marks

⬭ misspelling

⊙ add a period

= make a capital letter

Why is my ant so special? She is the one person in my famly who can do everything. She can fix a car. She is a great cook. She tells funny stories to my broter and sistre.

1. _____

2. _____

3. _____

4. _____

 MEANING STRATEGY Paragraph Plan to write a paragraph about a special person in your family. Think about what makes the person special. Choose and write at least three Core Words that you will use in your paragraph. Write your paragraph on a separate sheet of paper.

1. _____ 2. _____ 3. _____

Now proofread your word list and paragraph and correct any errors.

30 Review for Lessons 25–29

Lesson 25

Lesson 25
frog
trade
broom
free
brag
trick

PRONUNCIATION STRATEGY Say each Core Word. Write two words that spell the /tr/ sound.

1. _____   2. _____

MEANING STRATEGY Write a Core Word that fits each group of words.

3. dust, sweep, _____   4. pond, _____

PRONUNCIATION STRATEGY Say each Core Word. Write a word that has the same vowel sound as these words.

5. cat, tag, _____   6. seat, bee, _____

Lesson 26

Lesson 26
spy
speed
spin
space
sled
slick

PRONUNCIATION STRATEGY Say each Core Word. Write two words that spell the /sp/ sound.

1. _____   2. _____

DICTIONARY STRATEGY Write a Core Word that fits each meaning.

3. something for riding on snow _____

4. very slippery _____

Review

Lesson 27
chickens
whales
seals
rabbits
zebras
ants

PRONUNCIATION STRATEGY Say each Core Word. Write three plural words that have two syllables.

1. _____   3. _____

2. _____

CONVENTIONS STRATEGY Write a Core Word to fit each picture clue. Each word means more than one.

4. _____   5. _____

Lesson 28

Lesson 28
road
meet
dye
rode
see
meat

PRONUNCIATION STRATEGY Say each Core Word. Write two words that sound alike.

1. _____   _____

2. _____   _____

VISUALIZATION STRATEGY Write the Core Word formed by adding, dropping, or changing one letter in each word.

3. seem _____   4. dyed _____

Review

Lesson 29

brother
family
uncle
father
aunt
baby

VISUALIZATION STRATEGY Write two Core Words that are family words that end in *y*.

1. _____   2. _____

MEANING STRATEGY Write the Core Word that goes with each word.

3. mother _____   5. sister _____

4. aunt _____

Spelling Strategy

THINK Look at the Core Word lists on pages 126–128. Choose two words that are the hardest for you to spell. Write the word and a strategy to help you remember how to spell each word. For example: You use a *broom* to sweep the *room*.

Words	Spelling Strategies
1.	
2.	

Review

 PROOFREADING STRATEGY **Read the story. Find three misspelled Core Words. Circle them and write them correctly.**

Proofreading Marks	
⬭	misspelling
☰	make a capital letter
⊙	add a period

    Did you see the friskey baby wales? They spin and speed near their famely in the sea   Meet me and we'll spy on them

1. _____ 2. _____ 3. _____

Now find two places where a period should be added. Use the correct proofreading mark to show where each period should be added.

MEANING STRATEGY Speech
Write a speech that could be given by someone running for a school office. Use at least four spelling words. First, write the spelling words that you want to use.

1. _____ 3. _____

2. _____ 4. _____

Now proofread your speech and correct any errors.

Review

SPELLING FUN Use the following Core Words from Lessons 25-29 to complete this puzzle.

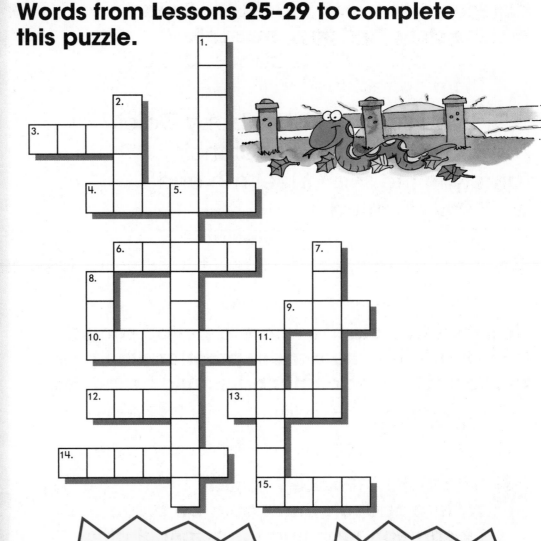

ACROSS

3. He _____ his bike.
4. The light is _____.
6. Rhymes with *brain*
9. A plant without water will do this.
10. Birds, fish, cows
12. Food from animals
13. Young child
14. Not a brother, a _____
15. _____ and slide

DOWN

1. The president gave a _____.
2. A male _____ has antlers.
5. Your mother's mother
7. Bouncy and playful
8. Ocean
11. Reptiles without arms or legs

Review

STANDARDIZED-FORMAT TEST PRACTICE

Choose the correct spelling of the Core Words from Lessons 25–29.

ANSWERS

SAMPLE	A. spie	B. spi	C. spy	Ⓐ Ⓑ Ⓒ
1.	A. brik	B. brick	C. bric	Ⓐ Ⓑ Ⓒ
2.	A. slied	B. slyde	C. slide	Ⓐ Ⓑ Ⓒ
3.	A. chickens	B. chikens	C. chickns	Ⓐ Ⓑ Ⓒ
4.	A. trick	B. chrick	C. trik	Ⓐ Ⓑ Ⓒ

Choose the misspelled Core Words from Lessons 25–29.

SAMPLE	A. trade	B. bruther	C. zebras	Ⓐ Ⓑ Ⓒ
1.	A. trane	B. slick	C. ducks	Ⓐ Ⓑ Ⓒ
2.	A. sister	B. cowse	C. dear	Ⓐ Ⓑ Ⓒ
3.	A. uncel	B. bright	C. slam	Ⓐ Ⓑ Ⓒ
4.	A. sea	B. brume	C. grandfather	Ⓐ Ⓑ Ⓒ

Choose the correct spelling of the Core Words from Lessons 25–29 to complete each sentence.

SAMPLE	Did you _____ that mouse?			
	A. see	B. sea	C. se	Ⓐ Ⓑ Ⓒ

1. The major made a _____.
   A. spech   B. speach   C. speech   Ⓐ Ⓑ Ⓒ

2. We saw a _____ in the forest.
   A. dear   B. deer   C. dere   Ⓐ Ⓑ Ⓒ

3. My _____ made me breakfast.
   A. mothr   B. muther   C. mother   Ⓐ Ⓑ Ⓒ

4. The _____ turned my shirt blue.
   A. dy   B. die   C. dye   Ⓐ Ⓑ Ⓒ

31 The /ŏŏ/ Sound

Spelling Focus—The /ŏŏ/ sound can be spelled *oo* or *u*.

VISUALIZATION STRATEGY Write the Core Words with the /ŏŏ/ sound spelled the following ways.

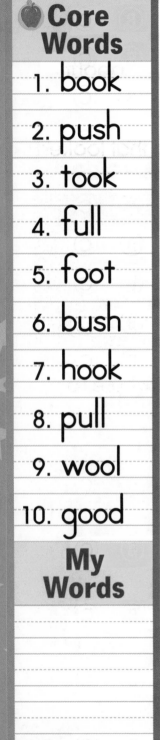

🍎 **Core Words**

1. book
2. push
3. took
4. full
5. foot
6. bush
7. hook
8. pull
9. wool
10. good

My Words

_____

_____

_____

_____

_____

_____

Core Word Sentences

We read the **book.**

Do not **push** the door.

He **took** the last apple.

The school bus is **full.**

One **foot** equals 12 inches.

Pick a flower off the **bush.**

I'll **hook** the leash to its collar.

Will you **pull** the wagon?

The **wool** sweater is warm.

She had a **good** idea.

4. _____

5. _____

6. _____

u

1. _____

2. _____

3. _____

4. _____

oo

1. _____

2. _____

3. _____

🍎 **WRITE** Write a sentence for each Core Word on a separate sheet of paper.

Spelling Words in Context

MEANING STRATEGY Write the Core Words that best complete the story. Use each word only once.

Another Fish Story

I went to the library to look for a _____ about

fishing. The shelves were _____ of books that looked

_____ _____ . I _____ one home.

The book tells how to tie on a _____ .

You learn to bring a _____ sweater and where to

put each _____ in a rowboat. I started to

_____ _____

_____ the oars toward me and then _____

them away from me. The boat did not move. It was still tied to

a _____ on the bank of the lake!

Core Words

1. book
2. push
3. took
4. full
5. foot
6. bush
7. hook
8. pull
9. wool
10. good

Challenge Words

brook

crook

shook

cookbook

stood

VISUALIZATION STRATEGY Fill in the missing letters to write the Core Words.

1. bu _ _ _____

2. pus _ _____

3. pul _ _____

4. fu _ _ _____

5. fo _ _ _____

6. ho _ _ _____

7. wo _ _ _____

8. bo _ _ _____

9. to _ _ _____

10. go _ _ _____

RHYMING STRATEGY Write the Challenge Words that fit these clues.

1. They rhyme with *cook.*

2. It rhymes with *hood.*

PROOFREADING STRATEGY Here is a draft of one student's paragraph about a book. Find three misspelled Core Words. Circle them and write them correctly.

Proofreading Marks

⬭	misspelling
⊙	add a period
=	make a capital letter

"Amelia Bedelia" is a funny buk. Amelia is a gud cook, but she gets things mixed up. She tuk some lightbulbs outside and hung them on a clothesline. I would like her as a friend!

1. _____

2. _____

3. _____

 MEANING STRATEGY Paragraph

Plan to write a paragraph describing a book you like. Think about why you like the book. Choose and write at least three Core Words that you will use in your paragraph. Write your paragraph on a separate sheet of paper.

1. _____   2. _____   3. _____

Now proofread your word list and paragraph and correct any errors.

32 Words with -ed or -ing

Spelling Focus—When *-ed* or *-ing* is added to words ending in a single consonant, the consonant is often doubled. Double the final consonant if the word has one syllable and one vowel.

Core Words

1. bat
2. mop
3. tapped
4. cutting
5. hit
6. tap
7. batting
8. mopped
9. hitting
10. cut

My Words

VISUALIZATION STRATEGY Write the Core Words that end with the following letters.

Core Word Sentences

Hit the ball with the **bat.**
I'll **mop** the floor.
He **tapped** on the door.
He is **cutting** patterns.
The movie is a big **hit.**
Now **tap** your toe.
We had **batting** practice.
She **mopped** the kitchen.
He kept **hitting** the nail.
I **cut** it in little pieces.

t

1. _____
2. _____
3. _____

-ed

1. _____
2. _____

-ing

1. _____
2. _____
3. _____

p

1. _____
2. _____

MEANING STRATEGY Write the Core Words that best complete the story. Use each word only once.

Hometown Hero

Our baseball game was tied. The coach _____

me on the shoulder. "You're next," she said. "Here's your _____."

I _____ my forehead with my sleeve.

I thought, "I am not very good at _____ the ball in

_____ practice. I should be home _____

the grass! I should tell the coach I have a _____ on my

hand." I tried to give the first pitch a little _____, but I

missed! Again, I had to _____ the sweat from my face.

Then I _____ a home run. The fans cheered!

Core Words

1. bat
2. mop
3. tapped
4. cutting
5. hit
6. tap
7. batting
8. mopped
9. hitting
10. cut

Challenge Words

running

skipping

hopping

digging

begged

VISUALIZATION STRATEGY Write the Core Words that fit these clues.

1. They end in *-ing.*

2. They end with *t.*

3. They end with *-ed.*

Add the underlined word parts together to make Challenge Words.

1. <u>beg</u>s + wag<u>ged</u> =

2. <u>sh</u>op + di<u>pping</u> =

3. <u>run</u>t + ow<u>ning</u> =

4. <u>dig</u>s + lo<u>gging</u> =

5. <u>skin</u> + cho<u>pping</u> =

PROOFREADING STRATEGY Here is a draft of one student's story about a lost game. Find three misspelled Core Words. Circle them and write them correctly.

Proofreading Marks

⬭	misspelling
⊙	add a period
=	make a capital letter

Last Game of the Season
    The game was tied. Then the catcher for the Tigers came to bot. He het a home run. I wished that I was at bat hiting the ball!

1. _____

2. _____

3. _____

 MEANING STRATEGY Story
Plan to write a story about a ball game. Think about a title for your story. Choose and write at least three Core Words that you will use in your story. Write your story on a separate sheet of paper.

1. _____   2. _____   3. _____

Now proofread your word list and story and correct any errors.

33 The /ou/ Sound

Spelling Focus—The /ou/ sound can be spelled *ou* or *ow*. It is most often spelled *ou*.

VISUALIZATION STRATEGY Write the Core Words with the following spellings.

Core Words

1. now
2. loud
3. down
4. house
5. clown
6. out
7. owl
8. sound
9. town
10. ouch

My Words

_____
_____
_____
_____
_____
_____

Core Word Sentences

Do your homework **now.**

The **loud** noise woke me.

Walk **down** the stairs.

A box can **house** our gerbil.

The **clown** made me laugh.

She walked **out** the door.

The **owl** hooted in the trees.

Please **sound** out the letters.

Our **town** is near a city.

I say **"ouch"** when I am hurt.

3. _____

4. _____

5. _____

ou

1. _____

2. _____

3. _____

4. _____

5. _____

ow

1. _____

2. _____

MEANING STRATEGY Write the Core Words that best complete the story. Use each word only once.

Come to the Circus

Listen, everybody! The circus has come to _____.

You can buy tickets from your _____.

Call right _____.

You will laugh at a funny _____

riding a horse. You will see two people shot _____

of a cannon. The _____ of the cannon blast is very

_____! I bet they say _____ when they

land! Then they will come _____ in a net. You can

see the show in the evening if you are a night _____.

Call today!

Building Spelling Vocabulary

**Core Words**

1. now
2. loud
3. down
4. house
5. clown
6. out
7. owl
8. sound
9. town
10. ouch

**Challenge Words**

found
around
south
howl
crown

VOWEL-SUBSTITUTION STRATEGY Add *ou* or *ow* to write the Core Words.

1. ___ ___ t

2. n ___ ___

3. s ___ ___ nd

4. t ___ ___ n

5. ___ ___ ch

6. l ___ ___ d

7. ___ ___ l

8. d ___ ___ n

9. h ___ ___ se

10. cl ___ ___ n

VISUALIZATION STRATEGY Do these word problems. Then write the Challenge Words.

1. h + fowl – f = _____

2. crowd – d + n = _____

3. f + sound – s = _____

4. s + mouth – m = _____

5. a + ground – g = _____

142   **The /ou/ Sound**

PROOFREADING STRATEGY **Here is a draft of one student's list of ways to make people laugh. Find three misspelled Core Words. Circle them and write them correctly.**

Proofreading Marks

⬯	misspelling
⊙	add a period
═	make a capital letter

Ways to Make People Laugh
1. Make a funny sownd.
2. Dress up like a cloun.
3. Hoot like an oul.

1. _____

2. _____

3. _____

 MEANING STRATEGY List
Plan to make a list of ways that you can make people laugh. Think about a joke or funny story you could tell. Choose and write at least three Core Words that you will use in your list. Write your list on a separate sheet of paper.

1. _____ 2. _____ 3. _____

Now proofread your word list and "laugh" list and correct any errors.

34 Compound Words

Spelling Focus—A compound word is two words put together to make one word. None of the letters are taken out of the words.

COMPOUND WORD STRATEGY Write the compound Core Words. Circle the two words that you find in each compound word.

Core Words

1. maybe
2. bedroom
3. lunchroom
4. notebook
5. doghouse
6. something
7. myself
8. nobody
9. into
10. inside

My Words

Core Word Sentences

Say yes, not **maybe.**

We swept the **bedroom.**

I ate in the **lunchroom.**

She has a **notebook.**

The **doghouse** is red.

I have **something** here.

I cleaned it **myself.**

There is **nobody** home.

He ran **into** the park.

What's **inside** the box?

3. _____

4. _____

5. _____

6. _____

7. _____

8. _____

1. _____

2. _____

9. _____

10. _____

MEANING STRATEGY Write the Core Words that best complete the story. Use each word only once.

School Days

On school days I get up early. There is _____

_____

else awake. I stay in my _____ and read for a

_____

while. Then I get dressed all by _____.

_____

I always have _____ to eat. Sometimes I

_____

have toast, or _____ cereal. My dog sleeps in the

_____

_____ at night. After breakfast I let him

_____

_____. I put my lunch, my pencil, and my

_____ _____

_____ _____ my backpack. My class

_____

eats in the _____. I pat my dog and off I go!

Core Words

1. maybe
2. bedroom
3. lunchroom
4. notebook
5. doghouse
6. something
7. myself
8. nobody
9. into
10. inside

Challenge Words

downtown

sailboat

sandbox

weekend

everywhere

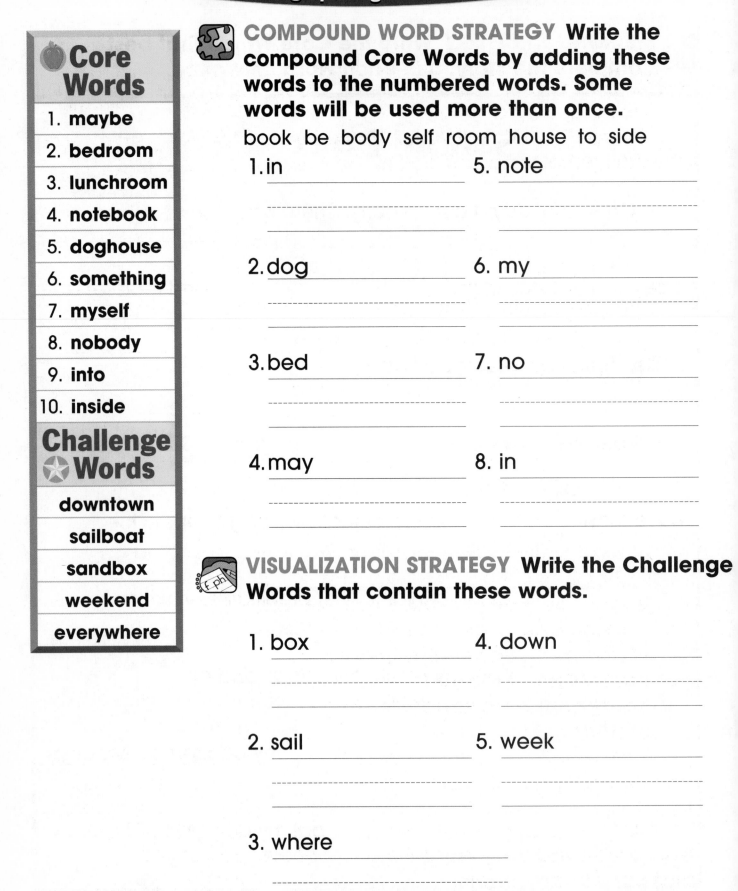

COMPOUND WORD STRATEGY Write the compound Core Words by adding these words to the numbered words. Some words will be used more than once.

book be body self room house to side

1. in _____

2. dog _____

3. bed _____

4. may _____

5. note _____

6. my _____

7. no _____

8. in _____

VISUALIZATION STRATEGY Write the Challenge Words that contain these words.

1. box _____

2. sail _____

3. where _____

4. down _____

5. week _____

PROOFREADING STRATEGY Here is a draft of one student's paragraph about a day at school. Find three misspelled Core Words. Circle them and write them correctly.

Proofreading Marks

⬭	misspelling
⊙	add a period
=	make a capital letter

I walked to school by miself. We ate lunch in the new lunchrum. Our teacher gave us a spelling notbook. I made a new friend.

1. _____

2. _____

3. _____

 MEANING STRATEGY Paragraph

Plan to write a paragraph about your first day of school this year. Think about how you felt and what you did. Choose and write at least three Core Words that you will use in your paragraph. Write your paragraph on a separate sheet of paper.

1. _____ 2. _____ 3. _____

Now proofread your word list and paragraph and correct any errors.

35 Number Words

Spelling Focus—Some words help you write about numbers.

Core Words

1. one
2. two
3. three
4. four
5. five
6. six
7. seven
8. eight
9. nine
10. ten

My Words

PRONUNCIATION STRATEGY Say each Core Word. Write the words that fit the following categories.

Core Word Sentences

He held up **one** hand.

I have **two** eyes.

She has **three** sisters.

The room has **four** walls.

I have **five** cents.

The band has **six** flutes.

Our home has **seven** rooms.

We live **eight** miles away.

Five plus four is **nine.**

A dime is **ten** cents.

one syllable

1. _____

_____

2. _____

3. _____

4. _____

5. _____

6. _____

7. _____

8. _____

9. _____

two syllables

1. _____

WRITE Write a sentence for each Core Word on a separate sheet of paper.

MEANING STRATEGY Write the Core Words that best complete the math problems. Use each word only once.

Just the Numbers, Please

Ten students in the class were divided into two teams. Five children were on each team. Here are the ten math problems they had to solve:

Two plus five is _____. Three plus five is

_____. Six take away four is _____. Seven take

away six is _____. Four plus six is _____.

Nine take away four is _____. Three plus one is

_____. Eight take away five is _____.

Two plus four is _____. Six plus three is _____.

Each student had to give the answer to one problem. How many would you have gotten right?

Core Words

1. **one**
2. **two**
3. **three**
4. **four**
5. **five**
6. **six**
7. **seven**
8. **eight**
9. **nine**
10. **ten**

Challenge Words

add

minus

second

count

numbers

VISUALIZATION STRATEGY Write the Core Words formed by adding, dropping or changing one or more letters in each word.

1. too _____

2. tin _____

3. tree _____

4. fine _____

5. won _____

6. for _____

7. even _____

8. line _____

9. sight _____

10. fix _____

Write the Challenge Words hidden in these letters.

1. plnumbersxr _____

2. addtqfr _____

3. xkmwminus _____

4. tzcountlh _____

5. vjlpsecond _____

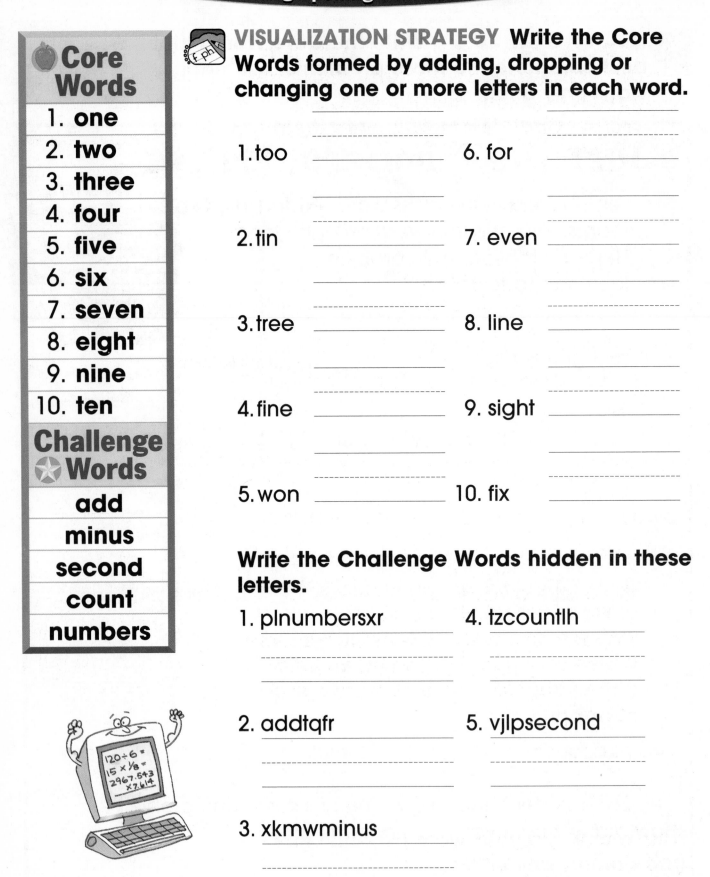

PROOFREADING STRATEGY Here is a draft of one student's story about her family. Find four misspelled Core Words. Circle them and write them correctly.

Proofreading Marks
⬭ misspelling
⊙ add a period
＝ make a capital letter

I am sevin years old. There are for children in my family. I have won brother and two sisters. When I am eiyht years old, I will get a new pet. I hope it is a dog.

1. _____

2. _____

3. _____

4. _____

 MEANING STRATEGY Story
Plan to write a story about yourself. Think about what you would like other people to know about you. Choose and write at least three Core Words that you will use in your story. Write your story on a separate sheet of paper.

1. _____ 2. _____ 3. _____

Now proofread your word list and story and correct any errors.

36 Review for Lessons 31–35

Lesson 31

Lesson 31

full
book
pull
took
push
bush

RHYMING STRATEGY Write two Core Words that rhyme with *bull*.

1. _____   2. _____

MEANING STRATEGY Write a Core Word to complete each sentence. The missing word will rhyme with the underlined word.

3. To press on a little tree is to <u>push</u> a _____.

4. At the library you <u>look</u> for a _____.

Lesson 32

Lesson 32

tap
mop
tapped
cutting
mopped
hit

VISUALIZATION STRATEGY Write two Core Words that spell the ending *-ed*.

1. _____   2. _____

MEANING STRATEGY Write a Core Word to complete each sentence.

3. I hope I can _____ the baseball as well as she does.

4. He is _____ the grass now.

Review

Lesson 33

ouch
town
owl
loud
house
sound

VISUALIZATION STRATEGY Write two Core Words that spell the /ou/ sound for the pattern *ou.*

1. _____   2. _____

Unscramble and write the underlined Core Words in these sentences.

_____

3. The <u>low</u> in the tree hooted at night. _____

4. The car made a <u>dlou</u> noise when it started.

_____

Lesson 34

Lesson 34

inside
maybe
notebook
nobody
lunchroom
into

COMPOUND WORD STRATEGY Write the compound Core Words that begin with *in.*

1. _____   2. _____

DICTIONARY STRATEGY Write a Core Word that fits each meaning.

3. You eat here at school. _____

_____

4. You write things in it.

Review

Lesson 35
five
two
nine
four
ten
six

PRONUNCIATION STRATEGY Say each Core Word. Write two number words that spell the /i/ sound.

1. _____   2. _____

VISUALIZATION STRATEGY Write a Core Word to answer each question using the pictures.

3. How many teeth?   _____

4. How many sides?   _____

Spelling Strategy

THINK Look at the Core Word list on pages 152–154. Choose two words that are the hardest for you to spell. Write each word and a strategy to help you remember how to spell each word. For example: You can find *us* in the *house*.

Words	Spelling Strategies
1. _____	_____
2. _____	_____

Review

 PROOFREADING STRATEGY Read the story. Find three misspelled Core Words. Circle them and write them correctly.

Proofreading Marks	
⬭	misspelling
＝	make a capital letter
⊙	add a period

"Ouch!" In the lunchroom, for full trays fell and hitt my foot. "don't be so lowd," said joe as he gave me a mop.

1. _____   2. _____   3. _____

Now find two words that should begin with a capital letter. Underline each letter three times to show it should be a capital letter.

 MEANING STRATEGY Announcement
Write an announcement for a special concert. Use at least four spelling words. First, write the spelling words that you want to use.

1. _____   3. _____

2. _____   4. _____

Now proofread your announcement and correct any errors.

Review

SPELLING FUN **Use the following Core Words from Lessons 31–35 to complete this puzzle.**

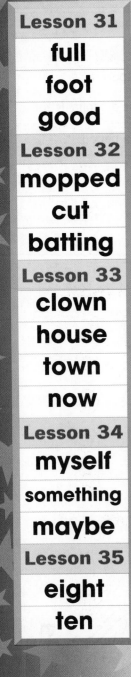

ACROSS

2. Circus performer
5. Swinging the bat
6. Right _____!
8. Thing not known
13. He _____ the floor.
14. Not empty

DOWN

1. Small city
2. Divide with a knife
3. Perhaps
4. Rhymes with *mouse*
7. This number rhymes with *late*.
9. My own self
10. After nine is _____.
11. We had a _____ time.
12. It has toes.

Review

Choose the correct spelling of the Core Words from Lessons 31–35.

ANSWERS

SAMPLE	A. loud	B. lowd	C. loude	Ⓐ Ⓑ Ⓒ
1.	A. pul	B. pull	C. pooll	Ⓐ Ⓑ Ⓒ
2.	A. down	B. doun	C. dowen	Ⓐ Ⓑ Ⓒ
3.	A. tapt	B. tappd	C. tapped	Ⓐ Ⓑ Ⓒ
4.	A. seven	B. sefen	C. sevn	Ⓐ Ⓑ Ⓒ

Choose the misspelled Core Words from Lessons 31–35.

SAMPLE	A. mopped	B. fiv	C. bush	Ⓐ Ⓑ Ⓒ
1.	A. hitting	B. three	C. sownd	Ⓐ Ⓑ Ⓒ
2.	A. bedroom	B. batt	C. hook	Ⓐ Ⓑ Ⓒ
3.	A. ouch	B. wull	C. mop	Ⓐ Ⓑ Ⓒ
4.	A. doghowse	B. myself	C. four	Ⓐ Ⓑ Ⓒ

Choose the correct spelling of the Core Words from Lessons 31–35 to complete each sentence.

SAMPLE	We went _____ when the rain came.			
	A. iside	B. insid	C. inside	Ⓐ Ⓑ Ⓒ

1. We _____ a walk in the park.
   A. tuk B. tuck C. took Ⓐ Ⓑ Ⓒ

2. The cat ran _____ the door.
   A. out B. owt C. oute Ⓐ Ⓑ Ⓒ

3. There was _____ at home.
   A. noboddy B. noebody C. nobody Ⓐ Ⓑ Ⓒ

4. I had only _____ piece of pie.
   A. won B. wun C. one Ⓐ Ⓑ Ⓒ

Often-Misspelled Words

Some words are hard to spell. They may not look the way they sound, or they may not follow spelling rules. This list shows some of these words. Study the words on this list. Learn how to spell them.

A
again
always
any
are

B
been

C
children
color
come
could

D
do
does
done

E
every

F
for
friend
from

G
give
goes
guess

H
have
her
here

I
I

L
live
love

M
many
my

N
nothing

O
of
once

S
said
school
shoe
some

T
the
their
they
to
too
trouble
two

V
very

W
want
was
were
where
who
work

Y
you
your

Structural Spelling Patterns

Plurals
- Add **–s** to most nouns to make them plural. (cat + s = cats)
- Add **–es** to words that end in *ch, sh, s, ss, x, z,* or *zz.*
- Noticing the syllables in the singular and plural forms of a word can help you know whether to add **–s** or **–es.** When **–es** is added, it usually adds another syllable.

Irregular Plurals
- For words that end in *f* or *fe,* change the *f* to a *v* and add **–es.**
- Some plurals are spelled the same as the singular form, such as *deer.*
- The spelling changes in the plural form of some words, like *tooth* and *teeth.*
- For a word that ends in **consonant-o,** add **–es.** If a word ends in **vowel-o,** **–s** is usually added.

Adding Endings
- For most words, endings are simply added to base words.
- If a word ends in *e* and the ending begins with a vowel, the *e* is dropped.
- When a word ends in **vowel-y,** just add the ending.

Continuous Stroke Handwriting Models

Aa Bb Cc Dd Ee Ff Gg

Hh Ii Jj Kk Ll Mm Nn

Oo Pp Qq Rr Ss Tt Uu

Vv Ww Xx Yy Zz

Aa Bb Cc Dd Ee Ff Gg

Hh Ii Jj Kk Ll Mm

Nn Oo Pp Qq Rr Ss Tt

Uu Vv Ww Xx Yy Zz

Ball and Stick Handwriting Models

Aa Bb Cc Dd Ee Ff Gg Hh

Ii Jj Kk Ll Mm Nn Oo Pp Qq

Rr Ss Tt Uu Vv Ww Xx Yy Zz

Aa Bb Cc Dd Ee Ff

Gg Hh Ii Jj Kk

Ll Mm Nn Oo Pp

Qq Rr Ss Tt Uu

Vv Ww Xx Yy Zz

Spelling Strategies

There are many different ways to learn how to spell. A spelling strategy is a plan or clue that can make learning to spell easier. These strategies appear in different lessons throughout this book. Take some time to learn how each one can help you to spell better.

SOUND PATTERN STRATEGIES

Pronunciation Strategy
Learn to listen to the sounds in a word. Then spell each sound.

sit

Consonant-Substitution Strategy
Try switching the consonant letters without changing the vowel.

bat, hat, rat, flat, splat/mat, mad, map, mask

Vowel-Substitution Strategy
Try switching the vowel letters without changing the rest of the word.

hit, hat, hut, hot/mane, mine/boat, beat

Rhyming Strategy
Think of a word that rhymes with the spelling word and has the same spelling pattern.

cub, tub, rub

STRUCTURAL PATTERN STRATEGIES

Conventions Strategy
Think about the rules and exceptions you have learned for adding endings to words.

crying, cried

Proofreading Strategy

Check your writing carefully for spelling mistakes you didn't mean to make.

Visualization Strategy

Think about how the word looks. Most words look wrong when they do not have the right spelling.

can not *cen*

MEANING PATTERN STRATEGIES

Family Strategy

Think of how words from the same family are spelled.

art, artist

Meaning Strategy

Think about the meaning of the word to make sure you're using the right word.

see, sea

Compound Word Strategy

Break the compound into its two words to spell each word.

homework, home work

Foreign Language Strategy

Think of foreign language word spellings that are different from English spelling patterns.

ballet

Dictionary Strategy

Find the word in a dictionary to make sure your spelling is correct.

How to Use a Dictionary

The word you look up in a dictionary is called the *entry word*. A dictionary tells you how to spell and pronounce the word. It also gives one or more definitions for the word.

The entry words in a dictionary are arranged in alphabetical order. If two words have the same first letter, they are put in alphabetical order using the second letter.

Study the dictionary entries below. Notice how much you can learn about a word from a dictionary.

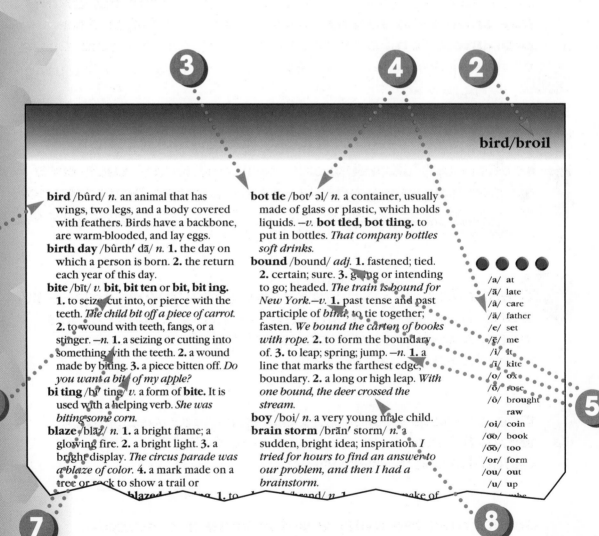

bird/broil

bird /bûrd/ *n.* an animal that has wings, two legs, and a body covered with feathers. Birds have a backbone, are warm-blooded, and lay eggs.

birth day /bûrth′ dā/ *n.* **1.** the day on which a person is born. **2.** the return each year of this day.

bite /bīt/ *v.* **bit, bit ten** or **bit, bit ing.**
1. to seize, cut into, or pierce with the teeth. *The child bit off a piece of carrot.*
2. to wound with teeth, fangs, or a stinger. —*n.* **1.** a seizing or cutting into something with the teeth. **2.** a wound made by biting. **3.** a piece bitten off. *Do you want a bite of my apple?*

bi ting /bī′ ting/ *v.* a form of **bite.** It is used with a helping verb. *She was biting some corn.*

blaze /blāz/ *n.* **1.** a bright flame; a glowing fire. **2.** a bright light. **3.** a bright display. *The circus parade was a blaze of color.* **4.** a mark made on a tree or rock to show a trail or

bot tle /bot′ əl/ *n.* a container, usually made of glass or plastic, which holds liquids. —*v.* **bot tled, bot tling.** to put in bottles. *That company bottles soft drinks.*

bound /bound/ *adj.* **1.** fastened; tied.
2. certain; sure. **3.** going or intending to go; headed. *The train is bound for New York.* —*v.* **1.** past tense and past participle of *bind,* to tie together; fasten. *We bound the carton of books with rope.* **2.** to form the boundary of. **3.** to leap; spring; jump. —*n.* **1.** a line that marks the farthest edge; boundary. **2.** a long or high leap. *With one bound, the deer crossed the stream.*

boy /boi/ *n.* a very young male child.

brain storm /brān′ storm/ *n.* a sudden, bright idea; inspiration. *I tried for hours to find an answer to our problem, and then I had a brainstorm.*

blazed, blazing. 1. to .... , **brand** /brand/ *n.* **1.** ..... make of

/a/	at
/ā/	late
/â/	care
/ä/	father
/e/	set
/ē/	me
/i/	it
/ī/	kite
/o/	ox
/ō/	rose
/ô/	brought
	raw
/oi/	coin
/ŏŏ/	book
/ōō/	too
/or/	form
/ou/	out
/u/	up

1 The *entry word* is the word you look up. Entry words are in bold type and are listed in alphabetical order. Sometimes there is more than one entry for a word. When this happens, each entry is numbered.

2 At the top of each dictionary page are two words called *guide words*. They are the first and last entry words appearing on that page. Guide words help you find an entry word quickly.

3 Words with more than one syllable are shown in parts. Spaces are used to show where words can be divided.

4 The *pronunciation* follows the entry word. It is given between two slashes. Special letters are used to show how to pronounce the word. A *pronunciation key* shows the sound for each special letter. The pronunciation key is found on each right-hand page of the dictionary.

5 The *part of speech* of the entry word is given after the pronunciation. Sometimes the part of speech is spelled out. Sometimes it is abbreviated, such as *n* for *noun* or *v* for *verb*. Some words can be more than one part of speech. If so, the dictionary may give a definition for each part of speech.

6 The dictionary also shows *irregular forms* of the entry word. If *–s, -es, -ed,* or *–ing* is simply added to the word, the dictionary does not list these regularly spelled forms.

7 One or more *definitions* are given for each entry word. If there is more than one definition, the definitions are numbered.

8 Sometimes the entry word is used in a *sample sentence or phrase* to help explain its meaning.

Speller Dictionary

···A····················

a cre /ā′ kər/ *noun, plural*
a cres. a measure of land
equal to 43,560 square feet.
*The farmer planted six acres
of corn.*

add /ad/ *verb* **add ed,
add ing. 1.** to find the sum
of two or more numbers. *If
you add 2 and 7, you will get
9.* **2.** to put in or on as
something extra. *We added a
porch to our house.*

aid /ād/ *verb* **aid ed, aid ing.**
to help out. *Doctors aid the
sick. —noun a help. The
woman asked for aid in
pushing the car.*

a larm /ə lärm′/ *noun, plural*
a larms. a bell, buzzer, or
other device used to wake
people up or to warn them of
danger. *Set the alarm for
seven o'clock.*

al mond /ä′ mund, am′ and/
noun, plural **almonds.** an
oval nut, the fruit of the
almond tree. *Walnuts and
almonds are good food.*

and /ənd, ən/ *conjunction* in
addition to. *The girls and
boys will read.*

an i mals /an′ ə məlz/ *noun*
plural of **an i mal. 1.** living
things that take in food and
move about and that are
made of many cells. Unlike
plants, animals do not have
to stay in one place, and they
cannot make their own food.
Jellyfish, worms, clams,
insects, birds, fish, mammals,
and human beings are all
animals. **2.** animals other
than humans. *My aunt and
uncle raise animals on
their farm.*

ants /ants/ *noun,* plural of
ant. small insects related to
bees and wasps. Ants live
together in large groups
called colonies.

an y /en′ ē/ *adjective* one or
some. *Sit in any chair.
—adverb* to any extent or
degree. *Are you feeling any
better? —pronoun* any one or
ones. *Any of these books is
sure to interest you.*

a pron /ā′ prən/ *noun, plural*
a prons. a piece of clothing
worn over the front of the
body to protect clothing. *The
baker wears a white apron.*

ar e a /âr′ ē a/ *noun, plural*
ar e as. a space or section.
*Please stay in the area close
to the house.*

arms /ärmz/ *noun* plural of
arm. 1. the parts of the body
between the shoulders and
the wrists. *He waved his
arms.* **2.** anything shaped like
an arm. *The arms of the
green chair are loose.*

a round /ə round′/ *adverb* **1.** in a circle. *The wheel spun around.* **2.** somewhere near. *Why not stay around for a few minutes.* —*preposition* in a circle or path that surrounds. *I wore a belt around my waist.*

art /ärt/ *noun, plural* **arts.** an activity by which one creates a work of beauty or special meaning. Painting, sculpture, composing, and writing are forms of art. Murals, ballets, and poems are works of art.

as /az/ *adverb* **1.** to the same degree or extent that. *They were proud as they could be.* **2.** in the same way or manner that. *Pronounce the word as I am pronouncing it.* —*preposition* in the manner, role, or function of. *I'm speaking to you as a friend.*

ask /ask/ *verb* **asked, ask ing.** to inquire. *We asked how to get to town.*

aunt /ant, änt/ *noun, plural* **aunts. 1.** the sister of one's mother or father. *The lady is one of my aunts.* **2.** the wife of one's uncle.

a way /ə wā′/ *adjective* **1.** distance. *The town is 3 miles away.* **2.** absent; gone. *My cousin has gone away.* —*adverb* **1.** from this or that place. *The frightened rabbit hopped away from the dog.* **2.** at a distance. *They stood far away from us.*

··B····················

ba by /bā′ bē/ *noun, plural* **ba bies. 1.** a very young child; infant. *The baby is learning how to walk.* **2.** the youngest person in a family or group. *I am the baby of the family.*

bad /bad/ *adjective* **worse, worst. 1.** having little quality or worth. *How can anyone watch such a bad television program?* **2.** not well or happy, especially because of regret or sadness. *I felt bad when we lost the game.* **3.** severe or violent. *He had a bad cold.*

bait /bāt/ *noun, plural* **baits.** food put on a hook or in a trap to attract and catch fish or other animals. *We use worms for bait.*

bal loon /bə lōōn′/ *noun, plural* **bal loons.** a rubber or plastic bag filled with air or gas. Small balloons are used as children's toys or for decoration. Large balloons are filled with hot air or some other very light gas so that they rise and float. These balloons have cabins or baskets for carrying passengers or scientific instruments.

/a/	at
/ā/	late
/â/	care
/ä/	father
/e/	set
/ē/	me
/i/	it
/ī/	kite
/o/	ox
/ō/	rose
/ô/	brought
	raw
/oi/	coin
/ŏŏ/	book
/ōō/	too
/or/	form
/ou/	out
/u/	up
/yōō/	cube
/ûr/	turn
	germ
	learn
	firm
	work
/ə/	about
	chicken
	pencil
	cannon
	circus
/ch/	chair
/hw/	which
/ng/	ring
/sh/	shop
/th/	thin
/ŧħ/	there
/zh/	treasure

band /band/ *noun, plural* **bands. 1.** a group of musicians playing together. *The band played at the game.* **2.** a strip of cloth or other material. *I tied a red band around my head.* **3.** a strip of another color. *A bumblebee has yellow and black bands on its body.*

barn /bärn/ *noun, plural* **barns.** a building on a farm that is used to store hay and grain and to house cows and horses. *The cows stay in the barn when it is cold.*

bat /bat/ *noun, plural* **bats.** a strong wooden stick or club. A bat is used to hit the ball in baseball and softball. —*verb* **bat ted, bat ting.** to use a bat in baseball and other games. *Our team will bat next.*

bath /bath/ *noun, plural* **baths** /baŧhz, baths/. **1.** a washing of something in water. *Give the dog a bath.* **2.** the water used for bathing. *The bath was too hot.*

bat ting /bat′ ing/ *verb* a form of **bat.** *He is batting the ball.*

be /bē/ *verb* **was** or **were, been, be ing.** to act, exist. *I will be at home on Saturday.*

bean /bēn/ *noun, plural* **beans.** a smooth and fairly flat seed, used as a vegetable. *I ate the last bean on my dinner plate.*

bears /bârz/ *noun* plural of **bear.** large, heavy animals with thick shaggy fur, sharp claws, and very short tails. Kinds of bears include the black bear, brown bear, and polar bear.

bed room /bed′ rōōm′, bed′ rŏŏm′/ *noun, plural* **bed rooms.** a room for sleeping.

begged /begd/ *verb* a form of **beg 1.** asked in a humble way. *The late guest begged to be excused.* **2.** asked in an eager or insisting way; plead. *The child begged to go to the rodeo.*

bend /bend/ *verb* **bent, bend ing. 1.** to change the shape of something by making it curved. *We will bend the wire.* **2.** to bow or stoop. *Bend over to tie your shoe.* **3.** *noun* a curve. *We came around a bend in the road.*

birch /bûrch/ *noun, plural* **birch es.** a tree that has hard wood. *The birch has thin white bark.*

bird /bûrd/ *noun, plural* **birds.** an animal that has wings, two legs, and a body covered with feathers. *Most birds can fly.*

blank /blangk/ *noun, plural* **blanks.** an empty space to be filled in. *Fill in the blank with your name.*

blan ket /blang′ kit/ *noun, plural* **blan kets.** a covering to use to keep warm while sleeping. *We used a warm blanket on our bed.*

blast /blast/ *noun, plural* **blasts.** an explosion. *The blast was loud.*

blast off /blast ôf/ *verb* **blast ed off, blast ing off.** to take off in flight propelled by a rocket. *We saw the spacecraft blast off.*

blaze /blāz/ *noun, plural* **blaz es. 1.** a bright flame. *We could see the blaze of the burning building.* **2.** a bright light. *We shielded our eyes from the blaze of the sun.*

blend /blend/ *verb* **blend ed, blend ing.** to mix together completely. *This drink blends fruit and ice cream.*

blimp /blimp/ *noun, plural* **blimps.** an airship that does not have a rigid shape. *I saw a blimp in the sky.*

blink /blingk/ *verb* **blinked, blink ing.** to close and open the eyes quickly. *Everyone blinked when they walked out of the dark into the light.*

blink er /blingk′ ər/ *noun, plural* **blink ers.** a blinking light used to send messages or give a warning. *The blinker goes on when the machine starts.*

block /blok/ *noun, plural* **blocks. 1.** a piece of something hard and solid, with flat surfaces. *The house was built of blocks of rock.* **2.** An area in a town or city with four streets around it. *We walk our dog around the block every morning.*

blood /blud/ *noun* the red liquid pumped by the heart. It carries food and oxygen and takes away wastes. *Blood came from the cut in her finger.*

blow /blō/ *verb* **blew, blown, blow ing. 1.** to move with speed or force. *An autumn breeze blew the leaves across the yard.* **2.** to send out a strong current of air. *Blow on your hands to warm them.*

boards /bordz/ *noun* plural of **board.** long, flat pieces of sawed wood. *Nail boards together to make a raft.*

boat /bōt/ *noun, plural* **boats. 1.** a small vessel that is used for traveling on water. A boat is moved by using oars, paddles, sails, or a motor. Passengers in boats usually sit in the open air. **2.** a ship. *An ocean liner is a boat.*

bon net /bôn′ ət/ *noun, plural* **bon nets.** a soft hat tied by strings under the chin. *Her plaid bonnet has a red ruffle.*

book /book/ *noun, plural* **books.** sheets of paper

/a/	at
/ā/	late
/â/	care
/ä/	father
/e/	set
/ē/	me
/i/	it
/ī/	kite
/o/	ox
/ō/	rose
/ô/	brought
	raw
/oi/	coin
/o͞o/	book
/o͞o/	too
/or/	form
/ou/	out
/u/	up
/yo͞o/	cube
/ûr/	turn
	germ
	learn
	firm
	work
/ə/	about
	chicken
	pencil
	cannon
	circus
/ch/	chair
/hw/	which
/ng/	ring
/sh/	shop
/th/	thin
/t͟h/	there
/zh/	treasure

fastened together between two covers. The pages of a book usually have writing or printing on them. *I like the pictures in these books.*

book keep er /book′ kēp ər/ *noun, plural* **book keep ers.** a person who keeps the records of a business. *The bookkeeper said the store made a big profit.*

book mak er /book′ māk ər/ *noun, plural* **book mak ers.** a person who prints or binds books. *The manuscript was taken to the bookmaker.*

boot /boot/ *noun, plural* **boots.** a covering for the foot and lower part of the leg. Boots are usually made of leather or rubber. —*verb* **boot ed, boot ing.** to kick. *The player booted the ball out of bounds.*

bored /bord/ *verb* a form of **bore.** made someone tired or restless by being dull. *You bored people by telling the same joke over and over.* —*adjective* weary or restless from something dull. *He was so bored that he fell asleep.*

bot tle /bot′ əl/ *noun, plural* **bot tles.** a glass or plastic container for liquids. *Buy three bottles of juice.*

bowl /bōl/ *noun, plural* **bowls.** a round dish that holds things. *Please put some milk in the cat's bowl.*

brag /brag/ *verb* **bragged, brag ging.** to speak with too much praise about what one does or owns; boast. *Stop bragging about how smart you are.*

bran /bran/ *noun, plural* **brans.** the outer part of wheat or other grains. *I have bran for breakfast.*

bread /bred/ *noun, plural* **breads.** a food made by mixing flour or meal with water or milk and then baking it in the oven. *We eat different types of bread.*

brick /brik/ *noun, plural* **bricks.** a block of clay baked in a kiln or in the sun. *Bricks are used in building.*

brief case /brēf′ kās/ *noun, plural* **brief cas es.** a flat case for carrying papers. *Her briefcase is made of black leather.*

bright /brīt/ *adjective* **bright er, bright est. 1.** giving much light. *The bright light of the sun hurt the swimmer's eyes.* **2.** clear, strong. *Let's paint the chair a brighter color.*

bring /bring/ *verb* **brought, bring ing. 1.** to cause something or someone to come with you. *Remember to bring your book home.* **2.** to cause something to come or happen. *The heavy rains will bring floods.*

brook /brŏŏk/ *noun, plural* **brooks.** a small, natural stream. *Let's fish in the brook.*

broom /brŏŏm, brŏŏm/ *noun, plural* **brooms.** a brush with a long handle, used for sweeping. *We used the broom to sweep up the dirt.*

broth er /bruth′ ər/ *noun, plural* **broth ers.** a boy or man having the same parents as another person. *The small boy is my brother.*

bruise /brŏŏz/ *noun, plural* **bruis es.** an injury that does not break the skin but leaves a blue-black mark. *I have a bruise on my arm from falling off my bike.*

bull /bŏŏl/ *noun, plural* **bulls.** the fully grown male of cattle. *The bull is kept apart from the quiet cows.*

bunch /bunch/ *noun, plural* **bunch es.** a number of things fastened together. *That is a big bunch of purple grapes.*

bush /bŏŏsh/ *noun, plural* **bush es.** a low-growing plant that often has many branches starting near the ground.

···C··················

cac tus /kak′ təs/ *noun, plural* **cac tus es** or **cac ti.** a plant with a thick stem covered with spines instead of leaves, found in desert areas. *That cactus is twenty feet tall.*

came /kām/ *verb* past tense of **come.** to reach a place; to arrive. *My friends came to my house.*

camp /kamp/ *noun, plural* **camps.** an outdoor place with tents where people sleep for a time. *The camp is near a river.* —*verb* **camped, camp ing.** to establish, equip, and live in a camp. *Last summer we camped in western Canada.*

cane /kān/ *noun, plural* **canes. 1.** a stick used to help someone walk. *I need a cane to walk.* **2.** another item shaped like such a stick. *I ate a candy cane.*

carp /kärp/ *noun, plural* **carp** or **carps.** a fish that lives in fresh water.

cart /kärt/ *noun, plural* **carts.** a strong wagon with two wheels that is used to carry a load. Carts are usually pulled by horses, mules, or oxen.

cash /kash/ *noun* money in the form of coins and paper bills. *Instead of paying for the coat with a check, I paid for it with cash.* —*verb* **cashed, cash ing.** to get or give cash for. *We have to cash a check at the bank.*

cask /kask/ *noun, plural* **casks.** a wooden barrel to

/a/	at
/ā/	late
/â/	care
/ä/	father
/e/	set
/ē/	me
/i/	it
/ī/	kite
/o/	ox
/ō/	rose
/ô/	brought
	raw
/oi/	coin
/ŏŏ/	book
/ōō/	too
/or/	form
/ou/	out
/u/	up
/yōō/	cube
/ûr/	turn
	germ
	learn
	firm
	work
/ə/	about
	chicken
	pencil
	cannon
	circus
/ch/	chair
/hw/	which
/ng/	ring
/sh/	shop
/th/	thin
/th/	there
/zh/	treasure

hold liquids. *The cellar held many casks of old wine.*

cast /kast/ *verb* **cast, cast ing.** the act of throwing. *We cast our fishing lines into the calm river.*

cel er y /sel′ ər ē/ *noun* a crisp, green vegetable.

cent /sent/ *noun, plural* **cents.** a coin. One hundred cents is equal to one dollar.

charm ing /chär′ ming/ *adjective* full of charm; pretty or nice. *The baby had a charming smile.*

chick /chik/ *noun, plural* **chicks. 1.** a baby chicken. **2.** a baby bird.

chick ens /chik′ ənz/ *noun* plural of **chicken.** birds that are raised on farms for their meat and eggs. Chickens may be of many different colors.

chief /chēf/ *noun, plural* **chiefs.** a leader of a group. *The chief of police will lead the parade.*

child /chīld/ *noun, plural* **chil dren.** a son or daughter. *The parents were very proud of their only child.*

chil dren /chil′ drən/ *noun,* plural of **child.**

chip munks /chip′ mungks/ *noun* plural of **chipmunk.** small animals that have brown fur with dark stripes on their backs and tails. Chipmunks are rodents and are related to squirrels.

choke /chōk/ *verb* **choked, chok ing.** to stop or hold back the breathing of by squeezing or blocking the windpipe. *That tight collar could choke the dog.*

chore /chor/ *noun, plural* **chores. 1.** a small job or task. *Feeding the cat is my chore.* **2.** a hard or unpleasant task.

church /chûrch/ *noun, plural* **church es.** a building where people gather for Christian worship. *Many families go to church on Sunday morning.*

churn /chûrn/ *noun, plural* **churns.** a container in which cream or milk is made into butter. —*verb* **churned, churn ing.** to stir or move with a forceful motion. *The water churned around the rocks at the bottom of the huge waterfall.*

clash /klash/ *noun, plural* **clash es.** a loud harsh sound like pieces of metal striking against each other. *The music ended with a clash of cymbals.* —*verb* to be in conflict. *Those colors clash.*

cloak /klōk/ *noun, plural* **cloaks.** a loose coat.

clown /kloun/ *noun, plural* **clowns.** a person who makes people laugh by playing tricks or doing stunts. A clown in a circus often wears funny clothing and makeup. *Clowns are funny.*

coach /kōch/ *noun, plural* **coach es. 1.** a large, closed carriage pulled by horses. A coach has seats inside for passengers and a raised seat outside for the driver. **2.** a teacher or trainer of athletes. *The basketball coach made the team practice extra hours.*

coal /kōl/ *noun, plural* **coals.** a fuel used to make heat or electricity.

coat /kōt/ *noun, plural* **coats. 1.** a piece of outer clothing with sleeves. *I have a new winter coat.* **2.** the outer covering of an animal. *Our dog has a shaggy brown coat.* **3.** layer. *The painters put on a new coat of paint on our house.*

con tracts /kən trakts´/ *verb* **con tract ed, con tract ing.** makes or becomes shorter or smaller. *A turtle contracts its neck to draw its head into its shell.* —*noun, plural* **con tracts.**

cook book /kook´ book´/ *noun, plural* **cook books.** a book of recipes and other information about food. *I looked in a cookbook to find out how to roast a turkey.*

cos tume /kos´ tōom, kos´ tyōom/ *noun, plural* **cos tumes.** clothes worn to look like someone or something else. *I wore a*

ghost costume to the Halloween party.

cot /kot/ *noun, plural* **cots.** a narrow bed. Cots usually have a frame that can be folded and put away.

count /kount/ *verb* **count ed, count ing.** to find out how many of something there are; add up. *Count the number of books on the highest shelf.*

cou sin /kuz´ in/ *noun, plural* **cou sins.** the son or daughter of an aunt or uncle.

cows /kouz/ *noun* plural of **cow. 1.** the fully grown females of cattle. Cows are raised for their milk, meat, and hide.

cream /krēm/ *noun, plural* **creams.** the yellowish white part of milk. *Butter is made from cream.*

crock /krok/ *noun, plural* **crocks.** a clay pot or jar.

crook /krook/ *noun, plural* **crooks. 1.** a bent part; curve. *I carry my umbrella in the crook of my arm.* **2.** a shepherd's staff with a hook at the top. **3.** a person who is not honest.

cross /krôs/ *adjective* **cross er, cross est.** in a bad temper; grouchy. *People sometimes get cross when you point out their mistakes.*

crown /kroun/ *noun, plural* **crowns.** a covering for the head worn by kings and

/a/	at
/ā/	late
/â/	care
/ä/	father
/e/	set
/ē/	me
/i/	it
/ī/	kite
/o/	ox
/ō/	rose
/ô/	brought
	raw
/oi/	coin
/ŏŏ/	book
/ōō/	too
/or/	form
/ou/	out
/u/	up
/yōō/	cube
/ûr/	turn
	germ
	learn
	firm
	work
/ə/	about
	chicken
	pencil
	cannon
	circus
/ch/	chair
/hw/	which
/ng/	ring
/sh/	shop
/th/	thin
/th/	there
/zh/	treasure

queens. A crown is often made of silver set with jewels. *The king has two crowns.*

cru el /krōō′ əl/ *adjective* **cru el er, cru el est.** willing to cause pain to others. *It would be cruel to beat an animal.*

cry /krī/ *verb* **cried, cry ing.** 1. to shed tears; weep. *The hungry baby cried.* 2. to call out loudly; shout. *The people in the burning building were crying loudly for help.*

cube /kyōōb/ *noun, plural* **cubes.** a block with square sides.

cut /kut/ *noun, plural* **cuts.** an opening or slit made with something sharp. *The cut on my foot was made by broken glass.* —*verb* **cut, cut ting** 1. to divide, pierce, open, or take away a part with something sharp. *We could not untie the knot so we had to cut the string.* 2. to make by using a sharp tool. *We cut a hole in the door so the cat could come in and go out.*

cut ting /kut′ ing/ *verb* a form of **cut.** *He was cutting down the tree.*

...D...................

dark /därk/ *adjective* **dark er, dark est.** having little or no light. *The night was dark*

because the clouds were covering the moon.

dash /dash/ *verb* **dashed, dash ing.** 1. to move fast; rush. *We dashed to the waiting bus.* 2. to destroy or ruin. *Spraining my ankle dashed my hopes of running in the race.* —*noun, plural* **dash es.** 1. a fast movement or sudden rush. *When the rain began we made a dash for cover.* 2. a small amount that is added or mixed in. *Add a dash of salt to the barley soup.*

dear /dir/ *adjective* **dear er, dear est.** much loved. *This is my dearest friend.* —*noun, plural* **dears.** a much loved person. *You are a dear to come over and help.*

deep /dēp/ *adjective* **deep er, deep est.** 1. far from the surface. *I don't swim in the deep end of the swimming pool.* 2. great in degree; extreme. *The weary child fell into a deep sleep.*

deer /dir/ *noun, plural* **deer.** an animal that has hooves, chews its cud, and runs very fast. A male deer has antlers that are shed every year and grow back the next year.

de mand ing /di man′ ding/ *adjective* needing much care. *He is a very demanding person.* —*verb* **de mand, de mand ed.**

desk /desk/ *noun, plural* **desks.** a piece of furniture used for reading or writing. *There are four drawers in my desk.*

die /dī/ *verb* **died, dy ing.** to stop living; become dead. *The flowers died during the dry spell.*

dig /dig/ *verb* **dug, dig ging.** **1.** to break up or turn over the earth with a shovel, the hands, or claws. *Our dog likes to dig in the yard for bones.* **2.** to make or get by hollowing out or digging. *The settlers had to dig a well for water.*

dig ging /dig′ ing/ *verb* a form of **dig.** *She was digging a hole when she fell.*

din o saur /dī′ nə sor′/ *noun, plural* **din o saurs.** one of a large group of extinct reptiles that lived millions of years ago. Some dinosaurs were the largest land animals that have ever lived, and others were as small as cats.

dirt /dûrt/ *noun* mud, dust, or other material that makes something unclean. *The children washed the dirt off their hands before coming to dinner.*

dis cov er /dis kuv′ ər/ *verb* **dis cov ered, dis cov er ing.** to see or find out for the first time. *Marie and Pierre Curie discovered radium.*

dish /dish/ *noun, plural* **dish es.** a plate or shallow bowl used for holding food. *We set the table with our good china dishes.*

do /dōō/ *verb* **did, do ing.** **1.** to carry out or perform. **2.** to make or create.

dock /dock/ *noun, plural* **docks.** a platform where boats or ships are tied up. *We pulled the boat to the dock.*

does /duz/ *verb* a form of **do.** used with *she, he, it,* or the name of a person, place, or thing. *The artist does beautiful paintings.*

dog /dôg/ *noun, plural* **dogs.** an animal that has four legs and makes a barking noise. Dogs have claws and sharp teeth for eating meat. Dogs are related to coyotes, wolves, and foxes.

dog house /dôg′ hous′/ *noun, plural* **dog hous es.** a shelter built for a dog.

dor mi to ry /dor′ mi tor′ ē/ *noun, plural* **dor mi to ries.** a building with many bedrooms where students live.

down /doun/ *adverb* from a higher to a lower place. *The painter climbed down from the ladder.*

down town /doun′ toun′/ *adverb* to or in the main part or business district of a town. *We went downtown to see a*

/a/	at
/ā/	late
/â/	care
/ä/	father
/e/	set
/ē/	me
/i/	it
/ī/	kite
/o/	ox
/ō/	rose
/ô/	brought
	raw
/oi/	coin
/ōō/	book
/ōō/	too
/or/	form
/ou/	out
/u/	up
/yōō/	cube
/ûr/	turn
	germ
	learn
	firm
	work
/ə/	about
	chicken
	pencil
	cannon
	circus
/ch/	chair
/hw/	which
/ng/	ring
/sh/	shop
/th/	thin
/ŧh/	there
/zh/	treasure

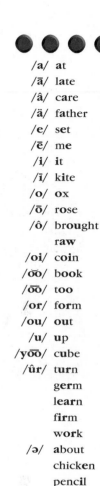

movie. — *adjective* located in the main part of town. *The downtown stores are larger than stores in our neighborhood.*

doze /dōz/ *verb* **dozed, doz ing.** to sleep lightly. *I dozed on the couch for an hour before supper.*

drag on /drag′ ən/ *noun, plural* **drag ons.** an imaginary beast that looks like a giant lizard with claws and wings.

dread ful /dred′ fəl/ *adjective.* **1.** very frightening; terrible. *The dreadful storm damaged many trees.* **2.** very bad; awful. *The movie was so dreadful that we left before it was over.*

dream /drēm/ *noun, plural* **dreams.** a series of thoughts, feelings, and apparent sights that a person has while asleep. *I had a dream that I was flying.* —*verb* to experience such a series.

dress /dres/ *noun, plural* **dress es.** a garment worn by a girl or a woman. *Joan has a new dress.*

drip /drip/ *verb* **dripped, drip ping.** to fall in drops. *Be careful not to drip paint on the rug.*

drive /drīv/ *verb* **drove, driv en, driv ing.** to operate and steer a car. *My teacher taught me to drive a car.*

drop /drop/ *verb* **dropped** or **dropt, drop ping. 1.** to move or fall down. *The wet dish dropped from my hand.* —*noun, plural* **drops. 1.** the act of dropping or falling. *The weather reporter said there would be a drop in temperature tonight.*

drove /drōv/ *verb* past tense of **drive.**

drum /drum/ *noun plural* **drums.** a musical instrument that is hollow and covered at the top and bottom with a material that is stretched tight. *My brother plays the drum at school.*

dry /drī/ *adjective* **dri er, dri est.** not wet or damp. *Cactuses grow well in a dry climate.*—*verb* to remove moisture from.

ducks /duks/ *noun* plural of **duck.** water birds that have broad bills and webbed feet that help them swim.

dump /dump/ *verb* **dumped, dump ing.** to drop, unload, or empty. *I dumped my books on the table.* —*noun* a place where trash is dumped.

dusk /dusk/ *noun* the time of day just before the sun goes down; twilight. *He worked in the fields from dawn to dusk.*

dust /dust/ *noun* tiny pieces of earth, dirt, or other matter. *The horse kicked up a cloud of dust.*

dye /dī/ *noun, plural* **dyes.** a substance that is used to give a particular color to hair, food, cloth or other materials. —*verb* **dyed, dye ing.** to color or stain something. *We dyed the blue curtains red.*

···E···················

each /ēch/ *adjective* every one of two or more things or persons thought of as individuals or one at a time. *Each player gets a turn.*

Earth /ûrth/ *noun* the planet on which we live.

ech o /ek′ ō/ *noun, plural* **ech oes.** the repeating of a sound. *After we shouted, we heard the echo of our voices .*

egg /eg/ *noun, plural* **eggs.** a round or oval body with a shell produced by chickens, birds, and other female animals. *I eat an egg once a week at breakfast.*

eight /āt/ *noun, plural* **eights.** one more than seven; 8. *Will eight hotdogs be enough?*

eight y /ā′ tē/ *noun, plural* **eight ies.** eight times ten; 80.

e las tic /i las′ tik/ *adjective* able to go back to its own shape soon after being stretched. Rubber bands and metal springs are elastic.

eve ry /ev′ rē/ *adjective* each person or thing of all the people or things that are part of a group. *Every student in the class is here.*

eve ry where /ev′ rē hwâr, ev′ rē wâr′/ *adverb* in every place; in all places. *Have you looked everywhere for the book you lost?*

ex pand /ek spand′/ *verb* **ex pand ed, ex pand ing.** to make larger or become larger. *Metal expands when it is heated.*

ex plore /ek splôr′/ *verb* **ex plored, ex plor ing.** to travel in unknown places for the purpose of discovery. *Astronauts explored the moon to learn what it is like.*

eye /ī/ *noun, plural* **eyes.** one of the organs of the body by which humans and other animals see or sense light. *I have brown eyes.*

···F···················

fam i ly /fam′ ə lē, fam′ lē/ *noun, plural* **fam i lies.** a group of people who are related. *The average family has three or four members.*

farm /färm/ *noun, plural* **farms.** a piece of land that is used to raise crops and animals. *The farm is near the small town.*

fast /fast/ *adverb* **fast er, fast est.** moving quickly. *A fast train rushed by.*

/a/	at
/ā/	late
/â/	care
/ä/	father
/e/	set
/ē/	me
/i/	it
/ī/	kite
/o/	ox
/ō/	rose
/ô/	brought
	raw
/oi/	coin
/o͝o/	book
/o͞o/	too
/or/	form
/ou/	out
/u/	up
/yo͞o/	cube
/ûr/	turn
	germ
	learn
	firm
	work
/ə/	about
	chicken
	pencil
	cannon
	circus
/ch/	chair
/hw/	which
/ng/	ring
/sh/	shop
/th/	thin
/t͟h/	there
/zh/	treasure

fa ther /fä′ ŧʰər/ *noun, plural* **fa thers.** a male parent. *My father is good to me.*

fed /fed/ *verb* past tense of **feed.** to give food to.

fif ty /fif′ tē/ *noun, plural* **fif ties.** five times ten; 50.

fight /fīt/ *noun, plural* **fights.** a struggle between animals, persons, or groups. *Two dogs had a fight over the bone.* —*verb* **fought, fight ing.** to struggle against; try to gain power over. *The firefighters fought the blaze for hours.*

find /fīnd/ *verb* **found, find ing. 1.** to discover or come upon by accident. *I found a wallet on the sidewalk.* **2.** to get or learn by thinking or calculating. *Please find the sum of this column of numbers.*

firm /fûrm/ *adjective* not giving in much when pressed; solid. *This is a very firm mattress.*

first /fûrst/ *adjective* before all others. *George Washington was the first president of the United States.* —*adverb* before all others. *She was ranked first in her class.*

fish /fish/ *noun, plural* **fish** or **fish es. 1.** a cold-blooded animal that lives in water. Fish have backbones, gills for breathing, and, usually, fins and scales. **2.** the flesh of fish used as food. —*verb* **fished, fish ing. 1.** to catch or try to catch fish. **2.** to search by groping. *I fished around in my pocket for the key.*

five /fīv/ *noun, plural* **fives.** one more than four; 5. *The child can count to five.*

fix /fiks/ *verb* **fixed, fix ing. 1.** to repair; mend. *I fixed the broken chair.* **2.** to get ready or arrange. *I will fix dinner.* —*noun, plural* **fix es.** trouble; difficulty. *I got myself into quite a fix by promising to go to two parties on the same evening.*

flash /flash/ *verb* **flashed, flash ing. 1.** to burst out in sudden light or fire. **2.** to come or move quickly. *The headlights of the car were flashing.* —*noun, plural* **flash es.** a sudden, short burst of light or flame. *A flash of lightning lit the sky for an instant.*

flight /flīt/ *noun, plural* **flights. 1.** movement through the air with the use of wings; flying. *We watched the graceful flight of the gull.* **2.** a trip in an airplane. *Did you have a good flight from Canada to New York?*

fling /fling/ *verb* **flung, fling ing.** to throw hard or carelessly. *Sometimes I just fling my coat on my bed.* —*noun, plural* **flings.** a throw. *I gave the pebble a fling and it landed in the pond.*

float /flōt/ *noun, plural* **floats. 1.** anything that rests on top of water. A raft anchored in the swimming area of a lake is a float. **2.** a low flat platform on wheels that carries an exhibit in a parade. *Our float won first prize in the parade.* —*verb* **float ed, float ing. 1.** to rest on top of water or other liquid. *In swimming class we learned how to float on our backs.* **2.** to move along slowly in the air or on water. *Far above us, a balloon floated.*

flop /flop/ *verb* **flopped, flop ping. 1.** to drop or fall heavily. *I couldn't wait to get home and flop into bed.* **2.** to fail completely. *The new restaurant flopped after being open only one month.* **3.** to move around or flap loosely. *The dog's ears flop when it runs.*

fly /flī/ *verb* **flew, flown, fly ing. 1.** to move through the air with wings. *Some birds fly south for the winter.* **2.** to pilot or travel in an aircraft. *The children flew to Puerto Rico to visit their grandparents.* **3.** to move, float. *I went to the park to fly my kite.*

fog /fôg, fog/ *noun, plural* **fogs.** a cloud of small drops of water close to the earth's surface. *The thick fog made driving dangerous.*

food /fōōd/ *noun, plural* **foods.** something that is eaten or taken in by people, animals, or plants that keeps them alive and helps them grow. *People and animals need food to live.*

foot /fōōt/ *noun, plural* **feet. 1.** the end part of the leg that humans and other animals walk or stand on. *We have two feet.* **2.** a measure of length equal to 12 inches. One foot is the same as 0.3048 meters.

foot man /fōōt′ mən/ *noun, plural* **foot men.** a male servant.

for /for/ *preposition* **1.** throughout a time or distance of. *We worked for two hours.* **2.** intended or reserved to keep. *This closet is for dishes.* **3.** with the purpose of. *She is studying for the test.*

for ty /for′ tē/ *noun, plural* **for ties.** four times ten; 40.

foul /foul/ *adjective* **foul er, foul est.** very unpleasant or dirty. *There was a foul odor in the air when the sewer pipes broke.*

found /found/ *verb* past tense of **find.**

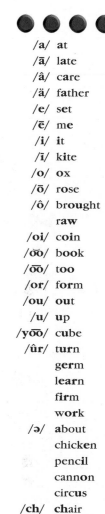

/a/	at
/ā/	late
/â/	care
/ä/	father
/e/	set
/ē/	me
/i/	it
/ī/	kite
/o/	ox
/ō/	rose
/ô/	brought
	raw
/oi/	coin
/ōō/	book
/ōō/	too
/or/	form
/ou/	out
/u/	up
/yōō/	cube
/ûr/	turn
	germ
	learn
	firm
	work
/ə/	about
	chicken
	pencil
	cannon
	circus
/ch/	chair
/hw/	which
/ng/	ring
/sh/	shop
/th/	thin
/t͟h/	there
/zh/	treasure

four /for/ *noun, plural* **fours.** one more than three; 4. *The four animals were in a pen.*

frac ture /frak′ chər/ *verb* **frac tured, frac tur ing.** to crack or break. *The hockey player fell and fractured an ankle.* —*noun, plural* **frac tures.** a crack or break. *With care, a fracture of a bone will usually heal.*

free /frē/ *adjective* **1.** having one's liberty; not under others' control. *We kept the injured bird until its wing healed, and then we set him free.* **2.** without cost or payment. *We received free tickets to the show.*

friend /frend/ *noun, plural* **friends.** a person whom one knows well and likes. *I like to play with my friends after school.*

frisk y /fris′ kē/ *adjective* **frisk i er, frisk i est.** playful; lively. *The puppy was frisky.*

frog /frôg, frog/ *noun, plural* **frogs.** a small animal with moist skin, webbed feet, and no tail. *Frogs are closely related to toads.*

frond /frond/ *noun, plural* **fronds.** the leaf of a fern.

front /frunt/ *noun, plural* **fronts. 1.** the part that faces forward or comes first. *This jacket has a zipper in the front.* **2.** a place or position ahead of the forward part. *He* entered the store while I waited in front.

frost /frôst/ *noun, plural* **frosts.** tiny ice crystals. *There was frost on the window this morning.*

fu el /fyo͞o′ əl/ *noun, plural* **fu els.** something that is burned to provide heat or power. Coal, wood, and oil are fuels.

full /fo͞ol/ *adjective* **full er, full est. 1.** holding as much or as many as possible. *I poured myself a full glass of milk.* **2.** having or containing a large number or quantity. *We had a house full of guests for the party.*

func tion /fungk′ shən/ *noun, plural* **func tions.** use or purpose. *The function of the heart is to pump blood through the body.*

G

gas /gas/ *noun* gasoline. *This car uses a lot of gas.*

get /get/ *verb* **got, got ten, get ting.** to come to have or own; receive; gain; earn. *I hope to get a radio for my birthday. I got a good grade on the test.*

girl /gûrl/ *noun, plural* **girls.** a female child from birth to the time she is a young woman. *There are ten girls in my class.*

give /giv/ *verb* **gave, giv en, giv ing.** to hand, pass, present, or grant. *My parents gave me a dog.*

glad /glad/ *adjective* **glad der, glad dest.** happy and pleased. *Our mother was glad we came home.*

glade /glād/ *noun, plural* **glades.** an open space in a forest.

glass /glas/ *noun, plural* **glass es.** a container used for drinking. *Please fill the glass with water.*

glide /glīd/ *verb* **glid ed, glid ing.** to move smoothly along without any effort. *The skater glided across the ice.*

globe /glōb/ *noun, plural* **globes.** 1. the world. *The group traveled around the globe and saw many interesting things.* 2. a round ball with a map of the world on it. *We studied the oceans and continents on a globe in our classroom.*

gloom /gloom/ *noun* dim light or darkness. *You can't see anything in the gloom of the forest at night.*

gloves /gluvz/ *noun* plural of **glove.** coverings for the hands. Most gloves have separate parts for each of the four fingers and for the thumb. However, boxing gloves and some baseball gloves hold four fingers together in one part. *I lost my gloves.*

glow /glō/ *noun, plural* **glows.** a light or shine. *At sunrise, the sky has an orange glow. A firefly gives off a glow.* —*verb* **glow ed, glow ing.** to shine or burn without catching on fire. *The light bulb in the hall glows brightly.*

glue /gloo/ *noun, plural* **glues.** a substance used for sticking things together. *Please use glue to put the vase back together.*

go /gō/ *verb* **went, gone, go ing.** to move or leave. *I go to school by bus.*

goat /gōt/ *noun, plural* **goats.** an animal that is related to the sheep. Goats have short horns and a tuft of hair under their chins that looks like a beard. They are raised in many parts of the world for their milk, hair, meat, and skin.

goes /gōz/ *verb* a form of **go.** used with *he, she, it,* or the name of a person, place, or thing. *That student goes to a piano lesson after school.*

good /good/ *adjective* **bet ter, best.** 1. of high quality; not bad or poor. *The food at this restaurant is good.* 2. nice or pleasant. *We had a good time.* 3. behaving properly. *The children were good while*

/a/	at
/ā/	late
/â/	care
/ä/	father
/e/	set
/ē/	me
/i/	it
/ī/	kite
/o/	ox
/ō/	rose
/ô/	brought
	raw
/oi/	coin
/oo/	book
/oo/	too
/or/	form
/ou/	out
/u/	up
/yoo/	cube
/ûr/	turn
	germ
	learn
	firm
	work
/ə/	about
	chicken
	pencil
	cannon
	circus
/ch/	chair
/hw/	which
/ng/	ring
/sh/	shop
/th/	thin
/ŧh/	there
/zh/	treasure

you were gone. **4.** real; true; genuine. *I have a good excuse for being late.*

goose /gōōs/ *noun, plural* **geese.** a bird that swims. Geese have webbed feet and are larger than ducks.

got /got/ *verb* past tense of **get.** *I got a birthday card in the mail yesterday.*

grand /grand/ *adjective* **grand er, grand est.** large and splendid. *The king and queen live in a grand palace.*

grand daugh ter /gran′ dô tər/ *noun, plural* **grand daugh ters.** a daughter of one's son or daughter.

grand fa ther /grand′ fä′ ŧhər/ *noun, plural* **grand fa thers.** the father of one's mother or father. *My grandfather will push the swing.*

grand moth er /grand′ muŧh′ ər/ *noun, plural* **grand moth ers.** the mother of one's mother or father. *The song is one that my grandmother taught me.*

grand pa /grand′ pä′, gram′ pə/ *noun* the father of one's mother or father; grandfather.

grand son /grand′ sun′/ *noun, plural* **grand sons.** a son of one's son or daughter.

grape /grāp/ *noun, plural* **grapes.** a small, juicy, round

fruit that grows on vines. *We like to eat grapes.*

graph /graf/ *noun, plural* **graphs.** a drawing that shows the relationship between changing things. *The class drew a graph to show how the population of the United States had grown over one hundred years.*

grasp /grasp/ *verb* **grasped, grasp ing.** to take hold of firmly with the hand. *The batter grasped the handle of the bat and swung.*

grass /gras/ *noun, plural* **grass es.** any large number of plants that have narrow leaves. *The cow eats grass from the field.*

grass hop pers /gras′ hop′ ərz/ *noun* insects that have wings and long, powerful legs which they use for jumping.

gray /grā/ *noun, plural* **grays.** a color between black and white. *Color the sky gray.*

grin /grin/ *noun, plural* **grins.** a broad, happy smile. *He had a grin on his face when he won.* —*verb* **grinned, grin ning.** to smile broadly.

grow /grō/ *verb* **grew, grown, grow ing.** to become bigger. *That plant will grow quickly in the window.*

grump /grump/ *noun, plural* **grumps.** one you cannot please. *She is a grump until noon.* —*verb* **grumped, grump ing.** to talk of not being pleased. *Don't grump about the flat tire.*

gust /gust/ *noun, plural* **gusts.** a sudden, strong rush of wind or air. *A gust of wind lifted my hat off my head and carried it across the street.*

···H···············

hand /hand/ *noun, plural* **hands.** the end of the arm from the wrist down. *There are four fingers and a thumb on a hand.*

hard /härd/ *adverb* **1.** with effort or energy. *They worked hard on their homework.* **2.** with force or strength. *It rained so hard yesterday that the roads were flooded.* —*adjective* **hard er, hard est.** solid and firm to the touch. *I slipped and fell onto the hard rock.*

harm /härm/ *noun, plural* **harms. 1.** injury or hurt. *To make sure no harm would come to the children, their parents made them wear life jackets when they went sailing.* **2.** an evil; wrong. *The child saw no harm in lying or stealing.*

harm less /härm′ lis/ *adjective* not able to cause harm.

has /haz/ *verb* a form of **have.** used with *he, she, it,* and the name of a person, place, or thing. *My friend has a new bicycle.*

hat /hat/ *noun, plural* **hats.** a covering for the head.

have /hav/ *verb* **had, hav ing.** to hold in one's hand or keep. *I have the paper in my right hand.*

hay /hā/ *noun.* grass, alfalfa, or clover that is cut and dried to feed animals. *The farmer feeds hay to the cow.*

hel i cop ter /hel′ i kop′ tər/ *noun, plural* **hel i cop ters.** an aircraft with blades that turn fast to make it fly.

his /hiz/ *pronoun* the one or ones that belong to or have to do with him. *This book is mine and that book is his.* —*adjective* of, belonging to, or having to do with him. *His best friend lives next door.*

hit /hit/ *verb* **hit, hit ting. 1.** to give a blow to; strike. *The bully hit my friend.* **2.** to send by striking with a bat or racket. *The batter hit the ball over the fence.*

hit ting /hit′ ing/ *verb* a form of **hit.** *He is hitting the rug with a broom to clean it.*

hook /hŏŏk/ *noun, plural* **hooks.** a bent piece of metal,

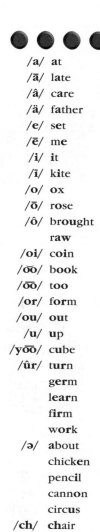

/a/	at
/ā/	late
/â/	care
/ä/	father
/e/	set
/ē/	me
/i/	it
/ī/	kite
/o/	ox
/ō/	rose
/ô/	brought raw
/oi/	coin
/ŏŏ/	book
/ōō/	too
/or/	form
/ou/	out
/u/	up
/yōō/	cube
/ûr/	turn germ learn firm work
/ə/	about chicken pencil cannon circus
/ch/	chair
/hw/	which
/ng/	ring
/sh/	shop
/th/	thin
/th/	there
/zh/	treasure

wood, or other strong material that is used to hold something. *There is a row of coat hooks along the wall in the classroom.* —*verb* **hooked, hook ing.** to hang, fasten, or attach with a hook. *We hooked the wire hanger over the nail.*

hop /hop/ *verb* **hopped, hop ping. 1.** to make a short jump on one foot. **2.** to move by jumping on both feet or all feet at once. *The frog hopped from one lily pad to another.*

hop ping /hop′ ing/ *verb* a form of **hop.** *Frogs were hopping in the grass.*

horn /horn/ *noun, plural* **horns. 1.** a hard, pointed growth on the head of some animals that have hooves. **2.** a device used to make a loud warning sound. *The bus driver honked the horn at the children.*

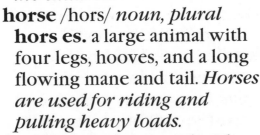

horse /hors/ *noun, plural* **hors es.** a large animal with four legs, hooves, and a long flowing mane and tail. *Horses are used for riding and pulling heavy loads.*

house /hous/ *noun, plural* **hous es.** a building in which people live; home. *Our friends asked us to come to their house for dinner.*

howl /houl/ *verb* **howled, howl ing.** to make a loud, wailing cry. Dogs and wolves both howl. *The wind howls when it blows hard.*

hush /hush/ *noun, plural* **hush es.** a silence or stillness that comes when a noise stops. *When the speaker raised his hand, there was a hush in the auditorium.*

··· I ····················

i de a /ī dē′ ə/ *noun, plural* **i de as.** a picture or thought formed in the mind. *The author had an idea for a new novel.*

if /if/ *conjunction* **1.** in case; in the event that; supposing that. *If I hurt your feelings, I'm sorry.* **2.** with the requirement or agreement that. *I can go to the movies if I finish my homework first.*

inch /inch/ *noun, plural* **inches.** a measure of length. Twelve inches equal one foot.

in side /in′ sīd′, in sīd′, in′ sīd′/ *noun, plural* **in sides.** the inner side or part; interior. *The inside of the house was dark.*

in to /in′ tōō, in′ tə/ *preposition* **1.** to or toward the inside of. *We ran into the house when it started to rain.* **2.** to make contact with. *The child bumped into the open door.*

...J...

jack al /jak′ əl/ *noun, plural* **jack als.** an animal that looks like a small dog.

jack et /jak′ it/ *noun, plural* **jack ets.** a short coat. *Our team wears jackets with the name of our team on the back.*

jam /jam/ *noun, plural* **jams.** a sweet food made by boiling fruit and sugar together until it is thick. Jam is used as a spread on bread and other foods.

job /job/ *noun, plural* **jobs.** **1.** a position of work; employment. *Did you get a job for the summer?* **2.** work that has to be done. *It's my job to feed and walk the dog every morning.*

jog /jog/ *verb* **jogged, jog ging.** to run or move at a slow, steady pace. *My parents jog in the park every morning for exercise.* —*noun* the act of jogging. *She likes to take a jog in the park.*

jump /jump/ *verb* **jumped, jump ing.** to use a push from one's feet to move through or into the air. *He had to jump to catch the ball.*

just /just/ *adverb* **1.** by very little. *Because of the traffic, you just missed the plane.* **2.** only, simply. *We saw them just yesterday.*

...K...

kan ga roos /kang′ gə rōōz′/ *noun,* plural of **kangaroo.** animals that have small front legs, very strong back legs for leaping, and long powerful tails for balance. The female kangaroo carries her young in a pouch for about six months after birth.

key /kē/ *noun, plural* **keys.** a shaped piece of metal that can open a lock. *We lost the key, so we can't unlock the front door.*

kick /kik/ *verb* **kicked, kick ing.** to hit with the foot. —*noun, plural* **kicks.** a hit or blow with the foot. *The child opened the door with a kick.*

kind /kīnd/ *adjective* **kind er, kind est.** gentle, generous, and friendly. *A kind person is thoughtful of other people.* —*noun, plural* **kinds.** a group of things that are the same in some way. *Blue whales are one kind of mammal.*

kiss /kis/ *verb* **kissed, kiss ing.** to touch with the lips as a sign of greeting or affection. *I kissed my aunt and uncle before they left.* —*noun, plural* **kiss es.** a touch with the lips. *The child gave her mother a kiss.*

knew /nōō/ *verb* past tense of **know.** to understand; be certain of the facts or truth of.

/a/	at
/ā/	late
/â/	care
/ä/	father
/e/	set
/ē/	me
/i/	it
/ī/	kite
/o/	ox
/ō/	rose
/ô/	brought
	raw
/oi/	coin
/o͝o/	book
/o͞o/	too
/or/	form
/ou/	out
/u/	up
/yōō/	cube
/ûr/	turn
	germ
	learn
	firm
	work
/ə/	about
	chicken
	pencil
	cannon
	circus
/ch/	chair
/hw/	which
/ng/	ring
/sh/	shop
/th/	thin
/ŧh/	there
/zh/	treasure

Who knew the answer to the question?

...L................

la dy bugs /lā′ dē bugz′/ *noun* small, round, bright red or orange beetles with spots.

land /land/ *verb* **land ed, land ing.** to bring to the ground. *The pilot will land the plane.*

land fill /land′ fil′/ *noun* an area of land that has been filled in with garbage.

lap /lap/ *noun, plural* **laps.** the front part of the body between the waist and the knees of a person who is seated. *The girl sat on her grandmother's lap.*

lark /lärk/ *noun, plural* **larks.** a small songbird with gray-brown feathers.

last /last/ *adjective* coming at the end. *The baby is the last one to go to sleep. I was the last person in line.*

leave /lēv/ *verb* **left, leav ing.** to omit. *We didn't have enough onions for the stew, so I left them out.*

lend /lend/ *verb* **lent, lend ing.** to let a person have or use something for a while. *Please lend me your baseball glove for the game.*

less /les/ *adjective* not as much. *I have less work to do today than I had yesterday.*

let tuce /let′ is/ *noun.* a plant with large green or reddish leaves. *I like lettuce in my salad.*

light /līt/ *adjective* **light er, light est. 1.** having little weight; not heavy. *The empty box was light.* **2.** not great in force. *A light rain fell.* **3.** moving easily; graceful; nimble. *The children were the lightest on their feet.* —*noun, plural* **lights. 1.** the form of energy that makes it possible for us to see. *The sun gives off rays of light.* **2.** device that gives off light.

li ons /lī ənz/ *noun* plural of **lion.** large, strong animals of the cat family. The lion lives mainly in Africa and southern Asia. The male has long, shaggy hair around its neck, head, and shoulders.

list /list/ *noun, plural* **lists.** a series of words, numbers, or other things. *The spelling words are in a list.*

live /liv/ *verb* **lived, liv ing.** to be alive; have life. *He lived during the Middle Ages.*

liz ards /liz′ ərdz/ *noun* animals with a scaly body, four legs, and a long tail.

lock /lok/ *noun, plural* **locks.** a fastener for a door, window, or a chest. *The front door has a lock.* —*verb* **locked, lock ing.** to fasten with a lock. *Don't lock that door.*

log /lôg, log/ *noun, plural* **logs.** a piece of a tree cut with the bark still on. *The pioneer family used logs to build their cabin.*

long /lông/ *adjective* **long er, long est.** great length; not short. *It's a long way from our school to the lake.*

lose /lo͞oz/ *verb* **lost, los ing. 1.** to have no longer. *Did you lose your pencil?* **2.** to fail to win. *The team will lose the game.*

lost /lôst/ *verb* past tense of **lose.** *I lost my gloves.*

lot /lot/ *noun, plural* **lots. 1.** a great amount. *There are a lot of cars on this road.* **2.** a piece of land. *We play baseball on an empty lot.*

loud /loud/ *adjective* **loud er, loud est.** having a strong sound; not quiet. *The jet plane made a loud noise.* —*adverb* in a loud way. *We hear you loud and clear.*

luck /luk/ *noun* good fortune seeming to happen by chance. *Wish me luck!*

lump /lump/ *noun, plural* **lumps.** a shapeless piece of something; chunk. *The sculptor took the lump of clay and made a figure of a dog with it.*

lunch /lunch/ *noun, plural* **lunch es.** a meal between breakfast and dinner. *They eat lunch at school.*

lunch room /lunch′ ro͞om′, lunch′ ro͝om′ / *noun, plural* **lunch rooms.** a place where light meals are served, especially a cafeteria in a school.

···M···············

mad /mad/ *adjective* **mad der, mad dest.** feeling or showing anger; angry. *I was mad when I found a scratch on my new bicycle.*

man /man/ *noun, plural* **men.** an adult male person. *The boy grew up to be a handsome man.*

man y /men′ ē/ *adjective* **more, most.** made of a large number. *There are many books on American history.* —*noun* a large number. *The meeting of the club was canceled because many of the members could not be there.* —*pronoun* a large number of people or things. *Many were late for school because of the snow.*

map /map/ *noun, plural* **maps.** a drawing that shows the surface features of an area. Maps of large areas usually show cities, rivers, oceans, and other features. *He studied the map before he started the car's engine.*

march /märch/ *verb* **marched, march ing. 1.** to walk with regular, measured

/a/	at
/ā/	late
/â/	care
/ä/	father
/e/	set
/ē/	me
/i/	it
/ī/	kite
/o/	ox
/ō/	rose
/ô/	brought
	raw
/oi/	coin
/o͝o/	book
/o͞o/	too
/or/	form
/ou/	out
/u/	up
/yo͞o/	cube
/ûr/	turn
	germ
	learn
	firm
	work
/ə/	about
	chicken
	pencil
	cannon
	circus
/ch/	chair
/hw/	which
/ng/	ring
/sh/	shop
/th/	thin
/t͟h/	there
/zh/	treasure

steps as soldiers do. People who march walk in step with others in an orderly group. **2.** to move forward steadily. *Time marches on.*

mask /mask/ *noun, plural* **masks. 1.** a covering worn to hide or protect the face. *We wear masks at Halloween.* **2.** anything that hides or conceals.

may be /mā′ bē/ *adverb* possibly; perhaps. *I don't agree with you, but maybe you are right.*

meal /mēl/ *noun, plural* **meals.** the food served or eaten at one time. *Breakfast is the first meal of the day.*

mean /mēn/ *verb* **meant, mean ing. 1.** to have in mind; want to do or say. *I do not know what you mean by that remark.* **2.** to have a purpose; intent. *I didn't mean to bake the cake so long.* —*adjective* **mean er, mean est.** not kind. *It is mean to make fun of other people.*

meat /mēt/ *noun, plural* **meats.** the parts of an animal used for food. The flesh of a cow, pig, or lamb is meat.

meet /mēt/ *noun, plural* **meets.** a meeting or contest. *Our school won first prize in the swimming meet.* —*verb* **met, meet ing. 1.** to come to a place where one is facing

someone or something coming from another direction. *While walking downtown, they met a friend they hadn't seen in a long time.* **2.** to be introduced to. *I will meet my tutor today.* **3.** to keep an appointment with. *We'll meet you after school.*

mend /mend/ *verb* **mend ed, mend ing.** to put in good condition again. *Use glue to mend the dish.*

mess /mes/ *noun, plural* **mess es.** a disorderly condition; untidy. *Clean up the mess in your room.*

met /met/ *verb* the past tense and past participle of **meet.** *Have you met his friend?*

might /mīt/ *verb* an auxiliary verb that is used in the following ways: **1.** to express the past of *may. I asked my teacher if I might leave.* **2.** to say something is possible. *The story we heard might be true, but I'm not sure.* **3.** to ask permission. *Might I borrow your dictionary?* **4.** to offer a suggestion. *You might try using a pencil so that you can erase your mistakes.* —*noun* great strength or power. *Press down with all your might.*

milk /milk/ *noun.* a white liquid food produced by glands in female mammals.

The milk of all mammals is used to feed their babies. The milk of cows is used as food by people.

mi nus /mī′ nəs/ *preposition*
1. decreased by; less. *Ten minus seven is three.*
2. lacking; without. *The chair was minus a leg.*

mis takes /mis tāks′/ *noun* plural of **mistake.** things that are not correctly done. *I made two spelling mistakes on the test.*

mitt /mit/ *noun, plural* **mitts.** a type of glove used in baseball. Mitts have padding to protect a person's hand.

mix /miks/ *verb* **mixed, mix ing. 1.** to put two or more different things together. *We mixed yellow roses and white roses in the bouquet.* **2.** to blend, combine, or join. *Oil and water don't mix.* —*noun, plural* **mix es.** something that is made by mixing; mixture. *This cake was made from a packaged mix.*

moon /mo͞on/ *noun, plural* **moons.** a heavenly body that revolves around Earth from west to east once every 29½ days. The moon seems to shine because it reflects light from the sun.

moose /mo͞os/ *noun, plural* **moose.** a large, heavy animal related to the deer that live in forests in cold northern regions of North America, Europe, and Asia. The male moose has enormous, broad antlers.

mop /mop/ *noun, plural* **mops.** a cleaning device made of a bundle of yarn or cloth or a sponge attached to a long handle. *Please use the mop to wipe up the water.* —*verb* **mopped, mop ping.** to clean or dry with a mop or other absorbent item. *I mopped the floor.*

mopped /mopt/ *verb* past tense of **mop.**

more /mor/ *adjective* greater in number. *A gallon is more than a quart.* —*adverb* to a greater amount. *Be more careful.* —*noun* an extra amount. *Our dogs always want more to eat.*

morn ing /mor′ ning/ *noun, plural* **morn ings.** the early part of the day. Morning ends at noon. *I slept late some mornings.*

moth er /muth′ ər/ *noun, plural* **moth ers.** a female parent. *My mother is pretty and she is nice.*

much /much/ *adjective* great in amount or degree. *I don't have much money left after buying that gift.*

mud /mud/ *noun* soft, wet dirt. *She had mud on her new shoes.*

/a/	at
/ā/	late
/â/	care
/ä/	father
/e/	set
/ē/	me
/i/	it
/ī/	kite
/o/	ox
/ō/	rose
/ô/	brought
	raw
/oi/	coin
/o͝o/	book
/o͞o/	too
/or/	form
/ou/	out
/u/	up
/yo͞o/	cube
/ûr/	turn
	germ
	learn
	firm
	work
/ə/	about
	chicken
	pencil
	cannon
	circus
/ch/	chair
/hw/	which
/ng/	ring
/sh/	shop
/th/	thin
/th/	there
/zh/	treasure

mul ti ply /mul′ tə plī/ *verb* **mul ti plied, mul ti ply ing.** to add a number to itself a certain number of times. *If we multiply 2 times 4, we get 8.*

must /must/ *verb* an auxiliary verb that is used to express the following meanings: **1.** to be obliged to. *I must return this book.* **2.** to be forced. *People must eat to live.* **3.** to be likely to. *They must have forgotten.*

mus tard /mus′ tərd/ *noun, plural* **mus tards.** a sharp-tasting yellow paste for flavoring food.

my self /mī self′/ *pronoun* **1.** my own self. *I cut myself.* **2.** my usual, normal, or true self. *I haven't been myself since the accident.*

...N...................

needs /nēdz/ *verb* a form of **need.** lacks or requires. *He needs a new coat.* —*noun plural of* **need.** requirements.

neph ew /nef′ yo͞o/ *noun, plural* **neph ews.** the son of one's brother or sister.

nest /nest/ *noun, plural* **nests.** a home made by birds in which they lay eggs. *The sparrows made a nest in the old oak tree in my yard.*

niece /nēs/ *noun, plural* **niec es.** the daughter of one's brother or sister.

night /nīt/ *noun, plural* **nights.** the time when it is dark; time between the setting and rising of the sun. *The baby slept seven nights without crying.*

nine /nīn/ *noun, plural* **nines.** one more than eight; 9. *There are nine boys on the team.*

nine ty /nīn′ tē/ *noun, plural* **nine ties.** nine times ten; 90.

no bod y /nō′ bod′ ē/ *noun, plural* **no bod ies.** a person of no importance or rank. *When they forgot his birthday, he felt like a nobody.* —*pronoun* no person; no one. *I rang the doorbell, but nobody answered the door.*

note book /nōt′ bo͝ok′/ *noun, plural* **note books.** a book with blank pages for notes. *Children take notebooks to school with them.*

now /nou/ *adverb* **1.** at this time; at this moment. *My friends are at the beach now, while I'm here working.* **2.** without delay. *Eat your food now.*

num ber strip /num′ bər strip/ *noun, plural* **num ber strips.** a long, narrow piece of paper used to stand for a number.

num bers /num′ bərz/ *noun* plural of **number.** symbols or words that tell how many.

2, 5, 77, and 396 are numbers.

...O...

oath /ōth/ *noun, plural* **oaths.** a promise to tell the truth.

off /ôf/ *preposition* no longer on, attached to, or connected with; away from. *A button is off my jacket.* —*adverb* so as to be no longer on, attached, or connected. *I broke a piece of bread from the loaf.*

one /wun/ *noun, plural* **ones.** the first and lowest number; 1.

os trich /ôs′ trich, os′ trich/ *noun, plural* **os trich es.** a large bird that has a long neck, strong legs, and a small, flat head.

ouch /ouch/ *interjection* word said when a person is hurt.

our /our/ *adjective* of, belonging to, or having to do with us. *Our house is on Oak Street by the pond.*

out /out/ *adverb* away from the center or from inside. *Water gushed out when I turned on the faucet.*

owl /oul/ *noun, plural* **owls.** a bird that has a round head with large, staring eyes and a hooked bill, a short square tail, and soft feathers. Owls eat mice, snakes, and insects and usually hunt at night.

—**night owl.** a person who often stays up late.

...P...

pack /pak/ *verb* **packed, pack ing.** to press together. *Go pack your case.* —*noun, plural* **packs.** a group of things. *I see a large pack of wolves in the field.*

pail /pāl/ *noun, plural* **pails.** a round, open container with a flat bottom and a curved handle. *The children carry sand and water in the pails.*

pain /pān/ *noun, plural* **pains.** a feeling of being hurt. *The blister gave me pain in my foot.*

par ent /pâr′ ənt/ *noun, plural* **par ents. 1.** a father or mother. *The lady and man are my parents.* **2.** a living thing that has produced offspring. *That animal is the parent of the little pup.*

park /pärk/ *noun, plural* **parks.** a piece of land, often having benches, trees, paths, and playgrounds, used by people for enjoyment and recreation. *We play ball in the park near our home.*

par lor /pär′ lər/ *noun, plural* **par lors.** a room in a house used for entertaining. *The party was held in the parlor.*

part /pärt/ *noun, plural* **parts.** something less than the whole. *We liked the first part of the movie the best.*

/a/	at
/ā/	late
/â/	care
/ä/	father
/e/	set
/ē/	me
/i/	it
/ī/	kite
/o/	ox
/ō/	rose
/ô/	brought
	raw
/oi/	coin
/o͝o/	book
/o͞o/	too
/or/	form
/ou/	out
/u/	up
/yo͞o/	cube
/ûr/	turn
	germ
	learn
	firm
	work
/ə/	about
	chicken
	pencil
	cannon
	circus
/ch/	chair
/hw/	which
/ng/	ring
/sh/	shop
/th/	thin
/t͟h/	there
/zh/	treasure

past /past/ *adjective* time gone by. *Vacation is past.*

pat /pat/ *verb* **pat ted, pat ting.** to tap or stroke gently with the hand. *I pat my dog when she obeys.*

path /path/ *noun, plural* **paths.** a trail or way for walking. *We had to shovel a path through the snow to our garages.*

peach /pēch/ *noun, plural* **peach es.** a yellow-pink fruit with fuzzy skin that grows on a tree.

peak /pēk/ *noun, plural* **peaks.** a high mountain, or the pointed top of a high mountain. *We could see the snowy peak in the distance.*

pen /pen/ *noun, plural* **pens.** **1.** a tool for writing or drawing with ink. *Do the writing with pen and ink.* **2.** a small yard for animals such as pigs. —*verb* **penned, pen ning.** to shut in closely. *Pen the chicks in the barn for the night.*

per son /pûr′ sən/ *noun, plural* **per sons.** a man, woman, or child; human being. *Every ten years, the government takes an official count of every person living in this country.*

pi lot /pī′ lət/ *noun, plural* **pi lots.** a person who operates an aircraft.

pin /pin/ *noun, plural* **pins.** **1.** a short piece of wire with a pointed end, used for holding things together. **2.** an ornament or badge that has a clasp for attaching it to clothing. *I wore a pin in the shape of a heart on my collar.* —*verb* **pinned, pin ning.** to hold together with a pin or pins. *My dress was too long, so I pinned up the hem.*

pine /pīn/ *noun, plural* **pines.** an evergreen tree that has cones and leaves that look like needles. *The wood from a pine is used in building and in making turpentine.*

pitch er /pich′ ər/ *noun, plural* **pitch ers.** **1.** a container used for holding and pouring milk, water, and other liquids. **2.** a baseball player who throws the ball to the batter.

plan /plan/ *noun, plural* **plans.** a way of doing something that has been thought out ahead of time. *Our plan for climbing the mountain is to zigzag up the south slope.* —*verb* **planned, plan ning.** to think out a way of doing something ahead of time. *We planned the dinner so there would be plenty of food for everyone.*

plan et /plan′ it/ *noun, plural* **plan ets.** one of nine large heavenly bodies that orbit the sun. The planets in our solar system are Mercury, Venus, Earth, Mars, Jupiter, Saturn, Uranus, Neptune, and Pluto.

plan e tar y /plan′ i ter′ ē/ *adjective* having to do with planets. *The astronomer studied planetary motion.*

plank ton /plangk′ tən/ *noun* very small plants and animals that float in seas and lakes.

plate /plāt/ *noun, plural* **plates.** a flat or shallow dish. *Food is served or eaten from plates.*

plot /plot/ *noun, plural* **plots.** **1.** a secret plan. *The outlaws formed a plot to rob the stagecoach.* **2.** the main story in a book, play, or movie. *That movie has an exciting plot.* **3.** an area of ground. *We had our picnic on a grassy plot in the shade.*

plum /plum/ *noun, plural* **plums.** a soft, juicy fruit with a pit. *The tree has red plums.*

plumb er /plum′ ər/ *noun, plural* **plumb ers.** a person who puts in and repairs water and sewage pipes in buildings. *A plumber came to the house to connect the washing machine.*

plus /plus/ *preposition* with the addition of. *Three plus two is five.*

poke /pōk/ *verb* **poked, pok ing.** to push, often with something pointed. *Don't poke me with your elbow.* — *noun* a thrust or push. *She got a poke in the arm.*

pond /pond/ *noun, plural* **ponds.** a body of a small amount of water surrounded by land. *There are fish in the small pond.*

pool /pool/ *noun, plural* **pools.** a tank of water to swim in, either indoors or outdoors. *The people next door to us have a pool.*

poor /poor/ *adjective* **poor er, poor est.** having little money. *We are too poor to buy a boat.*

po ta toes /pə tā′ tōz/ *noun* plural of **po ta to.** thick, rounded vegetables.

print ing /prin′ ting/ *noun* writing in which the letters are separated. —*verb* **print, printed.** a form of **print.** **1.** to produce a text, picture, or design on a surface by applying inked type, plates, or blocks. **2.** to write using letters like those made by type.

pull /pool/ *verb* **pulled, pull ing.** to grab or hold something and move it forward or toward oneself. *Two horses pulled the wagon.*

push /poosh/ *verb* **pushed, push ing. 1.** to press on

/a/ at
/ā/ late
/â/ care
/ä/ father
/e/ set
/ē/ me
/i/ it
/ī/ kite
/o/ ox
/ō/ rose
/ô/ brought
　　 raw
/oi/ coin
/o͝o/ book
/o͞o/ too
/or/ form
/ou/ out
/u/ up
/yo͞o/ cube
/ûr/ turn
　　 germ
　　 learn
　　 firm
　　 work
/ə/ about
　　 chicken
　　 pencil
　　 cannon
　　 circus
/ch/ chair
/hw/ which
/ng/ ring
/sh/ shop
/th/ thin
/ŧh/ there
/zh/ treasure

something in order to move it. *I pushed the cart through the market.* **2.** to move forward with effort. *We had to push through the crowd.*

······**R**·················

rab bits /rab′ its/ *noun* plural of **rabbit.** small animals that have long ears, a short tail, and soft fur. Rabbits live in burrows that they dig in the ground.

rain bow /rān′ bō′/ *noun, plural* **rain bow.** a curve of red, orange, yellow, green, blue, indigo, and violet light seen in the sky.

raise /rāz/ *verb* **raised, rais ing. 1.** to move or cause to move to a higher position. *I raised the flag.* **2.** to stir up or bring about. *Someone raised a commotion. —noun, plural* **rais es.** an increase in amount. *The worker received a raise in pay.*

rake /rāk/ *noun, plural* **rakes.** a tool that has a long handle with teeth or prongs attached at one end. It is used to gather leaves or smooth earth. *Use the rake on the cut grass. —verb* **raked, rak ing.** to gather leaves.

ram /ram/ *noun, plural* **rams. 1.** a male sheep. *The ram has white wool.* **2.** a device used to butt against or force

something. *—verb* **rammed, ram ming.** to hit hard. *I saw the ball ram against the wall.*

reach /rēch/ *verb* **reached, reach ing. 1.** to arrive at; come to. *We reached the cabin after walking two miles.* **2.** to touch or grasp. *I can't reach the top shelf of the bookcase.*

rea son /rē′ zən/ *noun, plural* **rea sons.** a statement that explains something. *The student gave a reason for being late.*

res cue /res′ kyōō/ *noun, plural* **res cues.** to save or free. *The lifeguard rescued the drowning child.*

rest /rest/ *noun, plural* **rests.** a time to relax. *She took a rest after working. —verb* **rest ed, rest ing.** to be quiet or at ease. *The parents could not rest until they knew the children were home.*

rich /rich/ *adjective* **rich er, rich est. 1.** having much money, land, or other valuable things. *The rich family gave a lot of money to charity.* **2.** having a lot of something. *Our country is rich in natural resources.*

ride /rīd/ *verb* **rode, rid den, rid ing.** to sit on and be carried by something in motion, such as a horse. *I will ride a camel at the zoo.*

right /rīt/ *adjective* **1.** correct or true; free of mistakes. *The student gave the right answer.* **2.** just, moral, or good. *Telling the truth was the right thing to do.* **3.** of, on, or toward the side of the body that is to the east when it is facing north. —*adverb* soon; immediately. *We will go right after lunch.*

ring/ring/ *noun, plural* **rings.** a band of metal or other material in the shape of a circle. *I wear a ring on my finger.*

rip /rip/ *verb* **ripped, rip ping.** to tear or pull apart. *I ripped my pants on the fence.* —*noun, plural* **rips.** a torn place; tear. *You have a rip in your shirt.*

road /rōd/ *noun, plural* **roads.** a strip of pavement or cleared ground that people or vehicles use to go from one place to another. *The workers covered all the roads with rock.*

rob in /rob′ in/ *noun, plural* **rob ins.** a bird that lives in North America and Europe. The American robin has a reddish orange breast and a black head and tail. *A family of robins lives in the tree in our front yard.*

rock /rok/ *noun, plural* **rocks.** a piece of stone. *She picked up a rock.*

rock et /rok′ it/ *noun, plural* **rock ets.** a device that is driven through the air by a stream of hot gases that is released from the rear. *Rockets are used to propel spacecraft.*

rock slide /rok slīd/ *noun, plural* **rock slides.** the falling of rock down a hillside. *The rockslide blocked the mountain road.*

rode /rōd/ *verb* past tense of **ride.** *He rode the bus to the museum.*

room /rōōm, rŏŏm/ *noun, plural* **rooms. 1.** an area that is or may be taken up by something. *There was no room to park the car in the lot.* **2.** an area in a house or building that is separated or set off by walls. *Our house has seven rooms.*

route /rout, rōōt/ *noun, plural* **routes.** a road or other course used for travelling. *We drove along the ocean route to the beach.*

row /rō/ *verb* **rowed, row ing.** to use oars to make a boat move. *We rowed the boat. We liked rowing the big boat.* —*noun, plural* **rows.** a series of people or things in a line. *A row of trees was planted in front of the house.*

rub /rub/ *verb* **rubbed, rub bing.** to press something back and forth

/a/ at
/ā/ late
/â/ care
/ä/ father
/e/ set
/ē/ me
/i/ it
/ī/ kite
/o/ ox
/ō/ rose
/ô/ brought
   raw
/oi/ coin
/ŏŏ/ book
/ōō/ too
/or/ form
/ou/ out
/u/ up
/yōō/ cube
/ûr/ turn
   germ
   learn
   firm
   work
/ə/ about
   chicken
   pencil
   cannon
   circus
/ch/ chair
/hw/ which
/ng/ ring
/sh/ shop
/th/ thin
/th/ there
/zh/ treasure

with pressure. *Rub your hands with soap.*

rude /rōōd/ *adjective* **rud er, rud est.** having or showing bad manners. *I've never met such a rude person.*

rug /rug/ *noun, plural* **rugs.** heavy fabric used to cover a floor. *There is a rug in front of the fireplace.*

rule /rōōl/ *noun, plural* **rules.** an instruction that serves as a guide. *If you want to play the game, you have to follow the rules.*

run /run/ *verb* **ran, run, run ning. 1.** to go or cause to go quickly. *I ran for help when I saw the fire.* **2.** to read and follow the instructions in a program. *The computer is running that new program.*

run ning /run′ ing/ *verb* a form of **run.** *We are running to catch the bus.*

rush /rush/ *verb* **rushed, rush ing. 1.** to move or go quickly. *We'll have to rush or we'll be late.* **2.** to act or do in a hurry. *Don't rush your work or you'll make errors.*

rust /rust/ *noun.* a reddish brown or orange coating that forms on iron when it is exposed to moisture or air. *The gate has spots of rust.*

...S..............

sack /sak/ *noun, plural* **sacks.** a bag made of strong material. *Place the sack of potatoes on the floor.*

sail boat /sāl′ bōt′/ *noun, plural* **sail boats.** a boat that is moved by the wind blowing against its sail or sails. *We went on the lake in a sailboat.*

sand /sand/ *noun.* loose grains of tiny crushed rock. *The beach is made of sand.*

sand box /sand′ boks′/ *noun, plural* **sand box es.** a large, low box or enclosed area filled with sand for children to play in. *The men filled two sandboxes with clean sand for the children.*

say /sā/ *verb* **said, say ing. 1.** to speak or pronounce words. *What did you say?* **2.** to repeat. *The class said the pledge.*

sea /sē/ *noun, plural* **seas.** part of the large body of salt water that covers almost three-fourths of Earth's surface; ocean. *The crew struggled to keep the ship afloat in the rough seas.*

seals /sēlz/ *noun* plural of **seal.** sea animals that live in coastal waters and have flippers instead of feet. Seals spend some of their time on land.

seam /sēm/ *noun, plural* **seams.** a line formed by sewing together the edges of two or more pieces of cloth, leather, or other material. *One of the seams in this coat is coming apart.*

sec ond /sek′ ənd/ *adjective* next after the first. *I liked the movie better the second time I saw it.* —*noun, plural* **sec onds. 1.** a person or thing that is next in line after the first. *She was second in line.* **2.** one of the sixty equal parts of a minute. —*verb* **sec ond ed, sec ond ing.** to help or support. *Who will second the motion to end the class meeting?*

see /sē/ *verb* **saw, seen, see ing. 1.** to look or look at with the eyes. *I see better with glasses.* **2.** to understand. *I see what you mean.* **3.** to experience. *Those old shoes have seen much wear.*

seem /sēm/ *verb* **seemed, seem ing. 1.** to appear to be. *The dark clouds make it seem later than it is.* **2.** to appear to oneself. *I seem to have forgotten your name.*

seen /sēn/ *verb* past participle of **see.**

send /send/ *verb* **sent, send ing.** to cause to go, come, or be. *Send the card to the lady next door.*

set /set/ *verb* **set, set ting. 1.** to place; put. *Set your books on the table. The child set the toy horse on its feet.* **2.** a group of things or persons.

sev en /sev′ ən/ *noun, plural.* **sev ens.** one more than six; 7. *There are seven boys on the porch.*

sev en ty /sev′ ən tē/ *noun, plural* **sev en ties.** seven times ten; 70.

shack /shak/ *noun, plural* **shacks.** a small, roughly built cabin. *We play in the shack.*

shad ow /sha′ dō/ *noun, plural* **shad ows. 1.** a dark area or figure made when rays of light are blocked by a person or thing. *The child cast a shadow.* **2.** a slight amount; suggestion. *There is not a shadow of a doubt that they are lying.*

shake /shāk/ *verb* **shook, sha ken, sha king.** to move quickly up and down, back and forth, or side to side.

shale /shāl/ *noun* rock formed from mud that has hardened.

shall /shal/ *verb* an auxiliary verb that is used in the following ways: **1.** to express future actions and conditions. *I shall be happy to see you.* **2.** to express a requirement. *You shall do as I say.* **3.** to ask a question that

/a/	at
/ā/	late
/â/	care
/ä/	father
/e/	set
/ē/	me
/i/	it
/ī/	kite
/o/	ox
/ō/	rose
/ô/	brought raw
/oi/	coin
/o͝o/	book
/o͞o/	too
/or/	form
/ou/	out
/u/	up
/yo͞o/	cube
/ûr/	turn germ learn firm work
/ə/	about chicken pencil cannon circus
/ch/	chair
/hw/	which
/ng/	ring
/sh/	shop
/th/	thin
/th/	there
/zh/	treasure

extends an invitation or offers a suggestion. *Shall we dance?*

shame /shām/ *noun* **1.** a painful feeling caused by having done something wrong or foolish. *He felt shame for having cheated.* **2.** a thing to be sorry for. *It was a shame that our team lost.*

share /shâr/ *verb* **shared, shar ing. 1.** to use with another or others. *Two of us shared a tent.* **2.** to divide into portions and give to others as well as to oneself. *I shared my sandwich.*

shark /shärk/ *noun, plural* **sharks.** a large, dangerous fish with sharp teeth.

sharp /shärp/ *adjective* **sharp er, sharp est.** having an edge or point that cuts or pierces easily. *That knife has a sharp blade.*

sheep /shēp/ *noun, plural* **sheep.** an animal with a thick, heavy coat that is raised on farms for its wool and meat. *They made the wool of the sheep into yarn.*

shine /shīn/ *verb* **shone** or **shined, shin ing.** to give or reflect light. *The stars shine at night.*

shirt /shûrt/ *noun, plural* **shirts.** a piece of clothing worn on the upper part of the body. One kind of shirt has a collar, sleeves, and buttons down the front.

shock /shok/ *noun, plural* **shocks.** a sudden, violent upsetting of the mind or emotions. *The parents never got over the shock of their child's accident.* —*verb* to disturb the mind or emotions of. *They were shocked by his behavior.*

shone /shōn/ *verb* a past tense and past participle of **shine.** *The light shone in the window.*

shook /shŏŏk/ *verb* past tense of **shake.** *The house shook from the earthquake.*

shoot /shōōt/ *noun, plural* **shoots.** a new or young plant or stem. *The plant started from a small shoot.* —*verb* **shot, shoot ing. 1.** to hit with a bullet, arrow, or the like. *Hunters shoot deer with rifles.* **2.** to send forth from a weapon. *I shot an arrow at the target.* **3.** to come forth. *The bean plants are shooting up from the ground.*

shore /shor/ *noun, plural* **shores. 1.** the land along the edge of an ocean, lake, or large river. *We walked along the shore.* **2.** land. *The sailors were glad to be back on shore after the long voyage.*

short /short/ *adjective* **short er, short est.** not long or tall. *The grass is short. —adverb* in a sudden or unexpected way. *The horse stopped short, and the rider fell off.*

show ers /shou′ ərz/ *noun* plural of **shower.** brief falls of rain. *The forecast called for showers today.*

shut /shut/ *verb* **shut, shut ting. 1.** to block or cover an entrance; close. *We shut the window.* **2.** to become closed. *The door shut behind me.*

shy /shī/ *adjective* **shi er, shi est. 1.** not comfortable around other people. *The shy child wouldn't come into the room.* **2.** easily frightened. *Animals that live in the woods are usually too shy to get close to people.*

sick /sik/ *adjective* **sick er, sick est.** poor health. *My friend is sick with a cold.*

sigh /sī/ *verb* **sighed, sigh ing.** to make a long, deep breathing sound because of sadness, tiredness, or relief. *She sighed after the race was over.*

sight /sīt/ *verb* **sight ed, sight ing.** to see with the eyes. *The group finally sighted the cabin.* *—noun, plural* **sights. 1.** the power to see. *My glasses helped improve my sight.* **2.** the act of seeing. *I recognized you at first sight.* **3.** something that is worth seeing. *The sunset was a beautiful sight.*

sis ter /sis′ tər/ *noun, plural* **sis ters. 1.** a girl or woman with the same mother and father as another person. *I have two sisters.* **2.** a woman who belongs to a religious order. A nun is a sister in a religious order.

six /siks/ *noun, plural* **six es.** one more than five; 6. *We counted off the teams in sixes.*

six ty /siks′ tē/ *noun, plural* **six ties.** six times ten; 60.

skil let /skil′ it/ *noun, plural* **skil lets.** a shallow pan with a handle.

skip /skip/ *verb* **skipped, skip ping. 1.** to spring or bound along, hopping lightly on one foot and then on the other. *The children skipped down the path.* **2.** to jump or leap over. *We skipped rope in the playground.* **3.** to pass or leave out. *Skip the arithmetic problems you can't do.*

skip ping /skip′ ing/ *verb* a form of **skip.** *The girls are skipping rope.*

skunk /skungk/ *noun, plural* **skunks.** an animal of the weasel family that has a bushy tail and black fur with white stripes along its back.

sky /skī/ *noun, plural* **skies.** the space or air above Earth.

/a/	at
/ā/	late
/â/	care
/ä/	father
/e/	set
/ē/	me
/i/	it
/ī/	kite
/o/	ox
/ō/	rose
/ô/	brought
	raw
/oi/	coin
/ o͝o /	book
/ o͞o /	too
/or/	form
/ou/	out
/u/	up
/yo͞o/	cube
/ûr/	turn
	germ
	learn
	firm
	work
/ə/	about
	chicken
	pencil
	cannon
	circus
/ch/	chair
/hw/	which
/ng/	ring
/sh/	shop
/th/	thin
/ŧh/	there
/zh/	treasure

On clear days, the sky has a light blue color.

slam /slam/ *noun, plural* **slams.** a forceful and noisy closing or striking. *The door closed with a slam.* —*verb* **slammed, slam ming.** to collide or close with force and a loud noise. *Please don't slam the door.*

slant /slant/ *noun, plural* **slants.** a sloping direction, line, or surface. *Hang the picture straight, not on a slant.* —*verb* **slant ed, slant ing.** to run or slope away from a straight line. *The roof slants toward the ground.*

slate /slāt/ *noun* bluish gray rock that splits easily into thin layers.

slav er y /slā′ və rē/ *noun* the practice of owning slaves.

sled /sled/ *noun, plural* **sleds.** a wooden framework mounted on runners. *A sled is used to carry people or loads over the snow.*

sleep /slēp/ *noun* **1.** a time or condition of rest that occurs naturally and regularly in humans and other animals. **2.** a condition that resembles sleep. *The bear's sleep lasts almost all winter.*

sleet /slēt/ *noun* rain mixed with snow or ice. *Sleet makes the roads slippery and driving dangerous.*

slen der /slen′ dər/ *adjective,* **slen der er, slen der est.** not big around; thin. *Everyone in my family is slender.*

slick /slik/ *adjective* **slick er, slick est. 1.** smooth and shiny. *The horse had a slick coat.* **2.** smooth and slippery. *A newly waxed floor is slick.* —*noun, plural* **slicks.** a smooth or slippery place on a surface. *The boat left a slick of oil on the water.*

slide /slīd/ *noun, plural* **slides.** a smooth surface for sliding. *I like to use the slide at school.* —*verb* **slid, slid ing. 1.** to move or cause to move smoothly, easily, quietly. *My friend slid into the seat next to me.* **2.** to fall or move suddenly from a position. *The truck slid off the icy road into a ditch.*

slime /slīm/ *noun* a thin, sticky substance given off by some animals, such as snails.

slimy /slī′ mē/ *adjective* **slim i er, slim i est.** of, covered with, or like slime; disgusting. *Don't go in the slimy pond.*

slip /slip/ *verb* **slipped, slip ping.** to move suddenly from a position or to slide out of control. *The man slipped on the ice.*

slot /slot/ *noun, plural* **slots.** a narrow, straight opening or groove. *Put the coin in the slot.*

slow /slō/ *adjective* **slow er, slow est. 1.** acting, moving, or happening with little speed. *The student was slow to answer the question.* **2.** behind the correct time. *Your watch is slow.*

sly /slī/ *adjective* **sli er, sli est. 1.** clever and shrewd; crafty. *The sly thief was never caught.* **2.** mischievous in a playful way. *The fox is slier than the chicken. He is the sliest of all.*

small ish /smôl′ ish/ *adjective* somewhat small. *I have rather smallish hands.*

smart /smärt/ *adjective* **smart er, smart est.** clever or intelligent; bright. *She is a smart girl who does well in school.* —*verb* **smart ed, smart ing.** to hurt or sting. *Does that cut smart?*

snack /snak/ *noun, plural* **snacks.** a small amount of food or drink eaten between regular meals. *I had a snack after school.* —*verb* **snacked, snack ing.** to eat a small amount. *He snacked on carrots.*

snakes /snāks/ *noun* plural of **snake.** animals that have a long body covered with scales and no legs, arms, or wings. Snakes are reptiles that move by curving and

then straightening out their bodies.

sneeze /snēz/ *verb* **sneezed, sneez ing.** to put forth air from the nose and mouth in a sudden, violent way. *When I have a cold I sneeze.*

snort /snôrt/ *verb* **snort ed, snort ing.** to force air through the nose noisily. *The horse snorted and threw back its head.*

snout /snout/ *noun, plural* **snouts.** the front part of an animal's head, including the nose, mouth and jaws. *An alligator has a long snout.*

snow /snō/ *noun, plural* **snows.** soft, white crystals of ice that fall to Earth as precipitation. Snow is formed when water vapor freezes in the air.

soap /sōp/ *noun, plural* **soaps.** a substance used for washing and cleaning. Soap is usually made with fats and lye. Soaps are made in the form of bars, powders, and liquids.

sog gy /sog′ ē/ *adjective* **sog gi er, sog gi est.** very wet or damp; soaked. *The ground was soggy after the heavy rain.*

some thing /sum′ thing′/ *adverb* to some extent; somewhat. *Your house looks something like ours.* —*pronoun* a thing that is not

/a/	at
/ā/	late
/â/	care
/ä/	father
/e/	set
/ē/	me
/i/	it
/ī/	kite
/o/	ox
/ō/	rose
/ô/	brought
	raw
/oi/	coin
/o͝o/	book
/o͞o/	too
/or/	form
/ou/	out
/u/	up
/yo͞o/	cube
/ûr/	turn
	germ
	learn
	firm
	work
/ə/	about
	chicken
	pencil
	cannon
	circus
/ch/	chair
/hw/	which
/ng/	ring
/sh/	shop
/th/	thin
/t͟h/	there
/zh/	treasure

known or stated. *Something is wrong with our car.*

song /sông/ *noun, plural* **songs.** music with words or other vocal sounds. *The words of the song are pretty.*

soon /sōōn/ *adverb* **1.** in a short time. *Come to visit us again soon.* **2.** before the expected time. *The guests arrived too soon, and we weren't ready.*

sound /sound/ *noun, plural* **sounds.** what can be heard. —*verb* **sound ed, sound ing.** to pronounce. *He will sound out the word.*

south /south/ *adjective* toward or in the south. *A south wind was blowing.* —*noun* south is a direction. *South is one of the four main points of the compass.*

space /spās/ *noun, plural* **spac es. 1.** the area in which the whole universe exists. *The planet Earth and everything and everyone on it exist in space.* **2.** an empty place.

Spain /spān/ *noun* a country in southwestern Europe.

spark /spärk/ *noun, plural* **sparks.** a small bit of burning or glowing material. *Sparks fly off burning wood.*

speak /spēk/ *verb* **spoke, spo ken, speak ing. 1.** to use or utter words; talk. *The baby cannot speak yet.* **2.** to

make known or express an idea, fact, or feeling. *She always speaks the truth.*

speech /spēch/ *noun, plural* **speech es. 1.** the ability to use spoken words to express ideas, thoughts, and feelings. *Animals do not have the power of speech.* **2.** something that is spoken; talk. *The president's speech was broadcast on television.* **3.** a way in which someone speaks. *Your speech shows no trace of an accent.*

speed /spēd/ *noun, plural* **speeds. 1.** Quick or fast motion. *She ran with great speed and won the race.* **2.** the rate of motion. *He drove the car at a speed of forty miles per hour.* —*verb* **sped** or **speed ed, speed ing.** to go or cause to go quickly or rapidly. *I sped down the hill on my sled.*

spice /spīs/ *noun, plural* **spic es.** the seeds or other parts of certain plants that are used to flavor food. *Peppers, cloves, and cinnamon are spices.*

spin /spin/ *verb* **spun, spin ning. 1.** to turn quickly. *The child spun the top.* **2.** to make thin fibers into thread. *They spun the fibers into thread.* **3.** to make a web or cocoon. *Spiders spin webs.*

spoke /spōk/ *noun, plural* **spokes.** one of the rods or bars that connect the rim of a wheel to the hub. *The spoke was broken on the wheel of my bike.* —*verb* past tense of **speak.** *We spoke to each other in whispers.*

spoon /spo͞on/ *noun, plural* **spoons.** a utensil with a small, shallow bowl at one end of a handle. A spoon is used for eating, measuring, or stirring.

spores /sporz/ *noun* plural of **spore.** cells that can develop into a new organism. *Ferns, mushrooms, bacteria, and certain other living things grow from spores.*

spot /spot/ *noun, plural* **spots. 1.** a place. *That park is a pleasant spot for a picnic.* **2.** a mark or stain left by dirt, food, or other matter. *There is a spot of ketchup on your collar.*

spot light /spot′ līt/ *noun* a strong beam of light pointed at a person, place, or object.

sprain /sprān/ *verb* **sprained, sprain ing.** to injure a joint or muscle of the body by twisting or straining it. —*noun* an injury caused by spraining. *plural* **sprains.**

spy /spī/ *noun, plural* **spies.** a person who watches others secretly. *A person is sometimes hired as a spy by the government.* —*verb* **spied, spy ing.** to watch others secretly. *He was sent to spy on the enemy.*

stack /stak/ *noun, plural* **stacks.** pile, as of hay, grass, or straw, arranged in an orderly way. *The hay is in a big stack.* —*verb* to put into a stack.

stain /stān/ *noun, plural* **stains.** a mark or spot. *There is an ink stain on the carpet.*

stamp /stamp/ *noun, plural* **stamps.** a small piece of paper that is stuck on letters and packages for the mailing fee. *Put a stamp on my letter.*

stand /stand/ *verb* **stood, stand ing.** to be upright on one's feet. *Tom will stand and wait for the bus.*

state /stāt/ *noun, plural* **states.** land that is part of a country. *Hawaii is a state of the United States.* —*verb* **stat ed, stat ing.** to say or tell.

steed /stēd/ *noun, plural* **steeds.** a horse.

stem /stem/ *noun, plural* **stems.** the main part of a plant that supports the leaves and flowers. *The flower broke off its stem.*

stern /stûrn/ *adjective* **stern er, stern est.** harsh or strict. *Our parents became stern when they realized that we had lied to them.*

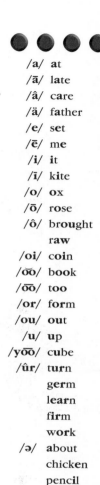

/a/	at
/ā/	late
/â/	care
/ä/	father
/e/	set
/ē/	me
/i/	it
/ī/	kite
/o/	ox
/ō/	rose
/ô/	brought
	raw
/oi/	coin
/o͝o/	book
/o͞o/	too
/or/	form
/ou/	out
/u/	up
/yo͞o/	cube
/ûr/	turn
	germ
	learn
	firm
	work
/ə/	about
	chicken
	pencil
	cannon
	circus
/ch/	chair
/hw/	which
/ng/	ring
/sh/	shop
/th/	thin
/t͟h/	there
/zh/	treasure

stick /stik/ *noun, plural* **sticks.** a thin, long piece of wood. *Put a stick of wood on the fire.* —*verb* **stuck, stick ing.** to put on or attach. *Stick the stamp on the letter.*

sting /sting/ *noun plural* **stings** a sharp pain or hurt. *Put lotion on that sting.* —*verb* **stung, sting ing.** to wound with a small, sharp point. *A bee will sting you.*

stood /stŏŏd/ *verb* past tense and past participle of **stand.** See **stand.**

store /stor/ *noun, plural* **stores. 1.** a place where goods are sold. *They went to the grocery store.* **2.** a supply of things put away for future use. *A store of firewood is in the garage.*

stout /stout/ *adjective* **stout er, stout est.** thick and heavy; fat. *The stout dog could barely climb the stairs.*

stripe /strīp/ *noun, plural* **stripes.** a long, narrow band. *Your shirt has red and white stripes.*

strong /strông/ *adjective* having great power or energy. *The weightlifter was very strong.*

stuck /stuk/ *verb* past tense of **stick.**

stuff y /stuf′ ē/ *adjective* **stuff i er, stuff i est.** without fresh air. *The room is stuffy; please open a window for fresh air.*

stump /stump/ *noun, plural* **stumps.** the lower part of a tree trunk that is left when the tree has been cut down.

sub trac tion /səb trak′ shən/ *noun, plural* **sub trac tions.** the taking away of one number from another number to find the difference. *5 – 2 = 3 is an example of subtraction.*

sun flow er /sun′ flou′ ər/ *noun, plural* **sun flow ers.** a large flower that grows on a tall plant. *A sunflower has a brown center and yellow petals.*

sus pend ers /sə spen′ dərz/ *plural noun* two straps worn over the shoulders to hold up trousers or a skirt.

sweet /swēt/ *adjective* **sweet er, sweet est.** having a taste like that of sugar or honey. *This apple is sweet and juicy.*

·· **T** ·····················

take /tāk/ *verb,* **took, tak en, tak ing. 1.** to get a hold of; grasp. *The student took a book from the shelf.* **2.** to capture or win by using force or skill. *My friend's painting took first prize.* **3.** to obtain; get. *The nurse took my temperature.* **4.** to carry with one; bring. *My parents took two suitcases on their trip.*

tap /tap/ *verb* **tapped, tap ping.** to hit or strike lightly. *I tapped out the beat to the music.*

tapped /tapt/ *verb* past tense of **tap.** *She tapped on my window to call me.*

task /task/ *noun, plural* **tasks.** work to be done. *The writing will be a small task.*

tax /taks/ *noun, plural* **tax es.** money that people or businesses must pay the government.

teach /tēch/ *verb* **taught, teach ing.** to help a person learn; show how. *My neighbor teaches swimming in a camp.*

team /tēm/ *noun, plural* **teams.** a group that plays, acts, or works together. *A team of scientists discovered a cure for the disease.*

ten /ten/ *noun, plural* **tens.** one more than nine; 10.

te pee /tē′ pē/ *noun, plural* **te pees.** a tent shaped like a cone. *North American Indians who lived on the plains used tepees.*

test /test/ *noun, plural* **tests.** a set of problems or tasks. *We have a spelling test on Friday.* —*verb* **test ed, test ing.** to give a test or to check. *The baker opened the oven and tested the bread.*

thank /thangk/ *verb* **thanked, thank ing. 1.** to say that one is grateful to. *I thanked the teacher for helping me.* **2.** to hold responsible. *I have you to thank for getting us into this mess.*

thick /thik/ *adjective* **thick er, thick est. 1.** having much space between one side or surface and another. *The outside wall of the building is thick.* **2.** growing or being close; dense. *The fog was thickest near the river.*

thin /thin/ *adjective* **thin ner, thin nest.** having little space between one side or surface and the other; not thick. *The thin wrapping paper did not hide the title of the book.*

thing /thing/ *noun, plural* **things. 1.** whatever is spoken of, thought of, or done. *That was an unkind thing to say.* **2.** the general state of affairs. *How are things at school?*

think /thingk/ *verb* **thought, think ing. 1.** to use the mind to form ideas or to make decisions. *Think carefully before you answer.* **2.** to have or form in the mind as an opinion, belief, or idea. *The teacher thought we were related.* **3.** to call to mind or remember. *I was thinking of my grandmother.*

/a/	at
/ā/	late
/â/	care
/ä/	father
/e/	set
/ē/	me
/i/	it
/ī/	kite
/o/	ox
/ō/	rose
/ô/	brought
	raw
/oi/	coin
/o͞o/	book
/o͞o/	too
/or/	form
/ou/	out
/u/	up
/yo͞o/	cube
/ûr/	turn
	germ
	learn
	firm
	work
/ə/	about
	chicken
	pencil
	cannon
	circus
/ch/	chair
/hw/	which
/ng/	ring
/sh/	shop
/th/	thin
/t͟h/	there
/zh/	treasure

third /thûrd/ *adjective* next after the second. *He was third in line.* —*noun, plural* **thirds.** one of three equal parts. *Cut the apple in thirds.*

thir ty /thûr′ tē/ *noun, plural* **thir ties.** three times ten; 30.

three /thrē/ *noun, plural* **threes.** one more than two; 3. *The three of us will play the game.*

thun der cloud /thun′ dər kloud′/ *noun, plural* **thun der clouds.** a dark cloud of great height that makes thunder and lightning.

tick /tik/ *noun, plural* **ticks.** a tiny animal that looks like a spider.

ti gers /tī gərz/ *noun* plural of **ti ger.** large animals that are members of the cat family. Most tigers have an orange or yellow coat with black or brown stripes. Tigers come from Asia.

tight /tīt/ *adjective* **tight er, tight est. 1.** held firmly; secure. *Make a tight knot so the string won't come loose.* **2.** made so that the parts are close together. *This sweater is very warm because it has such a tight knit.* **3.** fitting the body closely. *My belt was tight after I ate that big dinner.*

tip /tip/ *noun, plural* **tips. 1.** the end part or point. *The tips of the fingers are very sensitive.* **2.** a small piece that forms the end of something. *The cane had a shiny, rounded tip.*

tip toed /tip′ tōd′/ *verb* past tense of **tip toe.** walked quietly on the tips of one's toes. *I tiptoed out of the room so I wouldn't wake the baby.*

ti tle /tī′ təl/ *noun, plural* **ti tles.** the name of a book, painting, song, or other work of art.

to /tōō; *unstressed* tŏŏ, tə/ *preposition* **1.** in the direction of; toward. *Turn to the left.* **2.** on, upon, or against. *Tack the carpet to the floor.*

toad /tōd/ *noun, plural* **toads.** an animal that looks something like a frog. A toad has rough, dry skin and spends most of its time on land rather than water. Toads are amphibians.

toast /tōst/ *noun.* sliced bread that has been browned by heat. —*verb* **toast ed, toast ing.** to brown by heating. *We toast bread for breakfast.*

to geth er /tə geth′ ər/ *adverb* **1.** with one another. *The friends walked to school together.* **2.** into one gathering or mass. *Mix the butter and sugar together.*

3. in agreement or cooperation. *Let's work together to solve this problem.* **4.** considered as a whole. *Alaska is larger than Texas, California, and Montana together.*

too /to͞o/ *adverb* **1.** in addition; also. *I love to read, but I like movies, too.* **2.** more than is needed or wanted. *I am too short.*

took /to͝ok/ *verb* past tense of **take.**

tooth /to͞oth/ *noun, plural* **teeth.** one of the hard, white, bony parts of the mouth. Teeth are used for biting and chewing food and also in talking.

tor na do /tôr nā′ dō/ *noun, plural* **tor na does** or **tor na dos.** a powerful storm with winds that whirl in a dark cloud shaped like a funnel.

tow /tō/ *verb* **towed, tow ing.** to pull; to pull along. *The tugboat had to tow the boat to shore.*

tow er /tou′ ər/ *noun, plural* **tow ers.** a tall, narrow building or structure. *The castle had a huge tower.*

town /toun/ *noun, plural* **towns.** an area with buildings where people live and work. *A town is usually larger than a village but smaller than a city.*

trace /trās/ *verb* **traced, trac ing.** to copy by following lines seen through a piece of thin paper. *I traced the map so it would be exact.*

track /trak/ *noun, plural* **tracks.** **1.** a line of rails on which a car or train runs. *We walked beside the railroad track.* **2.** the mark or footprint of that which has passed. *We saw a track made by a deer.*

trade /trād/ *noun, plural* **trades.** **1.** the business of buying and selling goods. *The United States engages in much foreign trade.* **2.** the giving of one thing in return for something else. *The farmer makes trades of milk for eggs.* —*verb* to exchange one thing for another. *Let's trade lunches.*

trail /trāl/ *verb* **trailed, trail ing.** to follow behind. *The children trailed the parade.* —*noun, plural* **trails.** a path through an area. *They followed a marked trail.*

train /trān/ *noun, plural* **trains.** a line of railroad cars connected together. *Some trains carry passengers.* —*verb* **trained, train ing.** to teach to behave, think, or grow up in a certain way. *The parents trained their children to respect the rights of others.*

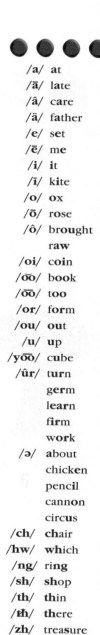

/a/	at
/ā/	late
/â/	care
/ä/	father
/e/	set
/ē/	me
/i/	it
/ī/	kite
/o/	ox
/ō/	rose
/ô/	brought raw
/oi/	coin
/o͝o/	book
/o͞o/	too
/or/	form
/ou/	out
/u/	up
/yo͞o/	cube
/ûr/	turn germ learn firm work
/ə/	about chicken pencil cannon circus
/ch/	chair
/hw/	which
/ng/	ring
/sh/	shop
/th/	thin
/t͟h/	there
/zh/	treasure

trait /trāt/ *noun, plural* **traits.** a quality of a person or animal; characteristic. *Bravery is a necessary trait for a firefighter.*

tramp /tramp/ *noun, plural* **tramps.** a person who wanders from place to place and has no home. *The tramp asked for food. –verb* **tramped, tramp ing. 1.** to walk or step heavily. *Don't tramp on the flowers.* **2.** to travel on foot; walk or hike. *They spent the day tramping through the woods.*

trap /trap/ *verb* **trapped, trap ping.** to catch in a trap. *Hunters trap tigers in a pit covered with branches.*

treat /trēt/ *noun, plural* **treats.** Something that is a special pleasure. *Going to the circus was a treat. –verb* **treat ed, treat ing.** to behave toward or deal with in a certain way. *The principal treated the student fairly.*

tree /trē/ *noun, plural* **trees.** a plant made of a single main stem. *A tree has branches and leaves.*

trick /trik/ *noun, plural* **tricks. 1.** an action done to fool or cheat someone. **2.** a clever or skillful act. *The magician pulled a rabbit out of a hat and did many other tricks. –verb* **tricked, trick ing.** to fool or cheat with a trick. *We tried to trick the teacher into letting us leave early.*

trim /trim/ *verb* **trimmed, trim ming.** to cut away parts to make things neat and orderly. *My dad will trim the hedge.*

trip /trip/ *verb* **tripped, trip ping.** to stumble or fall. *I tripped on the rug. –noun, plural* **trips.** the act of traveling. *We took a trip to Europe.*

trot /trot/ *verb* **trot ted, trot ting.** to move or ride at a medium pace. *The horse trotted toward the stable.*

truck /truk/ *noun, plural* **trucks.** a large motor vehicle used to haul things. *There are rocks in the truck.*

trunk /trungk/ *noun, plural* **trunks. 1.** the long snout of an elephant. **2.** the main stem of a tree. **3.** the baggage compartment of an automobile. **4.** a large box with a hinged lid, used to store things.

truth /trōōth/ *noun, plural* **truths.** something that is true. *They taught their children to tell the truth.*

try /trī/ *verb* **tried, try ing.** to make an effort. *I will try to do my best.*

try ing /trī′ ing/ *verb* form of **try.** It is used with a helping verb. *They were trying to build a treehouse.*

tube /tōōb, tyōōb/ *noun, plural* **tubes.** a hollow piece of glass, rubber, plastic, or metal in the shape of a long pipe, used to carry liquids or gases. *A garden hose is a long tube.*

tug /tug/ *verb* **tugged, tug ging.** to give a pull on something. *The horses tugged the heavy wagon. —noun, plural* **tugs.** a hard pull. *Suddenly I felt a tug on the fishing line.*

tune /tōōn, tyōōn/ *noun, plural* **tunes. 1.** a series of musical tones that form a pleasing, easily remembered unit. *We hummed the tune when we couldn't remember the words.* **2.** a song. *The band played a popular tune.*

twen ty /twen′ tē/ *noun, plural* **twen ties.** two times ten; 20.

twig /twig/ *noun, plural* **twigs.** a small branch of a tree. *We gathered dry twigs to start a campfire.*

twins /twinz/ *noun plural of* **twin.** two children or animals born at the same time to the same mother. *Some twins look exactly alike.*

two /tōō/ *noun, plural* **twos.** one more than one; 2. *There were two birds on the wire.*

···U····················

un cle /ung′ kəl/ *noun, plural* **un cles. 1.** the brother of one's mother or father. *My uncle will go with me.* **2.** the husband of one's aunt.

un der ground rail road /un′ dər ground rāl′ rōd/ *noun* a system that helped runaway slaves.

un der neath /un′ dər nēth′/ *preposition* in a lower place or position; below. *Pack the records on top and the books underneath.*

u nit /yōō′ nit/ *noun, plural* **u nits.** one part of something. *An hour is a unit of time.*

us /us/ *pronoun* the persons who are speaking or writing. *The neighbors invited us to dinner.*

···V····················

val ley /val′ ē/ *noun, plural* **val leys.** an area of low land between hills and mountains. *We hiked along the river in the valley.*

ver y /ver′ ē/ *adjective* mere; by itself. *The very idea of having to get up early makes me groan. —adverb* to a high degree. *I am very sorry that you are not feeling well.*

vi brate /vī′ brāt/ *verb* **vi brat ed, vi brat ing.** to

/a/	at
/ā/	late
/â/	care
/ä/	father
/e/	set
/ē/	me
/i/	it
/ī/	kite
/o/	ox
/ō/	rose
/ô/	brought
	raw
/oi/	coin
/ŏŏ/	book
/ōō/	too
/or/	form
/ou/	out
/u/	up
/yōō/	cube
/ûr/	turn
	germ
	learn
	firm
	work
/ə/	about
	chicken
	pencil
	cannon
	circus
/ch/	chair
/hw/	which
/ng/	ring
/sh/	shop
/th/	thin
/th/	there
/zh/	treasure

move rapidly; shake. *The strings of a guitar vibrate when they are plucked.*

····**W**··············

week end /wēk′ end′/ *noun, plural* **week ends.** the period of time from Friday night or Saturday morning until Sunday night or Monday morning. *We went to the country for the weekend.*

weigh /wā/ *verb* **weighed, weigh ing.** to find out the weight or heaviness of a person or thing. *The grocer weighed the tomatoes on a scale.*

went /went/ *verb* past tense of **go.** *We went to the lake to swim.*

were /wûr/ *verb* past tense of **be.** used with *you, we, they,* or the plural form of a noun. *We were at home all day.*

west /west/ *noun* the direction where the sun sets. *Look to the west to see the beautiful sunset.*

whales /hwālz, wālz/ *noun* plural of **whale.** large animals that have bodies like fish. Whales are found in all oceans and in certain fresh waters. Whales are mammals.

what /hwut, hwot, wut, wot/ *pronoun* **1.** used to ask questions about persons or things. *What is today's date?*

2. the thing that. *They knew what I was thinking.*

wheat /hwēt, wēt/ *noun* a kind of grass whose seeds are used to make flour and other foods.

wheel /hwēl, wēl/ *noun, plural* **wheels.** a round frame or solid object used on cars and wagons. *The car has four wheels.*

where /hwâr, wâr/ *adverb* in, at, to, or from what place. *Where did they go?*

while /hwīl/ *conjunction* during or in the time that. *Did anyone call while I was away?* —*noun* a period of time. *We rested for a while.*

whirl /hwûrl, wûrl/ *noun, plural* **whirls.** dizzy condition. *My head was in a whirl after I hit the ball.* —*verb* **whirled, whirl ing.** to turn or cause to turn quickly in a circle. *The blades of the fan are whirling.*

whisk /hwisk, wisk/ *verb* **whisked, whisk ing.** to move or carry quickly. *The taxi whisked us to the airport.*

whisk ers /hwis′ kərz, wis′ kərz/ *noun* plural of **whisker.** **1.** the hair growing on a man's face. *My dad has whiskers on his face before he shaves.* **2.** stiff hairs that grow on the face. *Cats and dogs have whiskers.*

whis per /hwis′ pər, wis′ pər/ *verb,* **whis pered, whis per ing.** to speak or say very softly. *My friend whispered a secret to me.* —*noun, plural* **whis pers.** a very soft spoken sound. *The teacher heard whispers from the back of the room.*

who /hoō/ *pronoun* **1.** what or which person or persons. *Who gave you that pen?* **2.** that. *The student who wrote that story has a good sense of humor.*

why /hwī, wī/ *adverb* for what reason or purpose. *Why are you laughing?*

wick /wik/ *noun, plural* **wicks.** a cord in an oil lamp or candle.

wide /wīd/ *adjective,* **wid er, wid est. 1.** made of or covering a large area from side to side. *There is a wide porch across the back of the house.* **2.** having a certain distance from side to side. *The room is 12 feet wide.* **3.** fully opened. *The child's eyes were wide with excitement.*

wind[1] /wind/ *noun, plural* **winds.** air moving over the earth. *The wind blew the tree over.*

wind[2] /wīnd/ *verb* **wound, wind ing. 1.** to roll into a ball. *I will wind this wool into a ball.* **2.** to turn in one direction or another. *The road winds around the mountain.*

wing /wing/ *noun, plural* **wings.** movable parts of the body used for flying. *The bird has a broken wing.*

wish /wish/ *noun, plural* **wish es. 1.** a feeling of wanting something; a strong desire. **2.** a thing that a person wants. *I hoped for a compass for my birthday, and I got my wish.* —*verb* **wished, wish ing.** to want something very much; have a wish. *I wish that summer would last longer.*

with /with, with/ *preposition* **1.** in the company or keeping of. *We went to the movie with friends.* **2.** having or possessing. *We need someone with good skills for the job.*

wolf /wŏolf/ *noun, plural* **wolves.** a wild animal that looks like a dog.

wood /wŏod/ *noun* the hard material that makes up the trunk and branches of a tree or bush. *We built a birdhouse out of wood.*

wool /wŏol/ *noun, plural* **wools.** the soft, thick, curly hair of sheep and some other animals such as the llama and alpaca. Wool is spun into yarn, which is made into cloth. *I have a sweater made from wool.*

/a/	at
/ā/	late
/â/	care
/ä/	father
/e/	set
/ē/	me
/i/	it
/ī/	kite
/o/	ox
/ō/	rose
/ô/	brought
	raw
/oi/	coin
/ŏo/	book
/ōo/	too
/or/	form
/ou/	out
/u/	up
/yōo/	cube
/ûr/	turn
	germ
	learn
	firm
	work
/ə/	about
	chicken
	pencil
	cannon
	circus
/ch/	chair
/hw/	which
/ng/	ring
/sh/	shop
/th/	thin
/th/	there
/zh/	treasure

...Y..................

yard /yärd/ *noun, plural* **yards.** an area of ground next to or surrounding a house, school, or other building. *We have a vegetable garden in the yard around our house.*

yet /yet/ *adverb* **1.** at the present time. *I have never yet been late.* **2.** after all the time that has gone by. *Are you ready yet?*

your /yŏor, yor; *unstressed* yər/ *adjective* of or belonging to you. *Let's meet tomorrow at your house.*

...Z....................

ze bras /zē′ brəz/ *noun* plural of **zebra.** wild animals that look like horses with black-and-white striped coats. Zebras come from southern and eastern Africa.

zip /zip/ *verb* **zipped, zip ping.** to close with a zipper. *Help me zip my coat.*

zip code /zip kōd/ *noun, plural* **zip codes.** a number written after the address on a piece of mail.

zoo /zōo/ *noun, plural* **zoos.** a park or public place where wild animals are kept for people to see. *The children went to the zoo to see the animals.*

zoom /zōom/ *verb* **zoomed, zoom ing. 1.** to move upward suddenly. *The wind made the kite zoom above the treetop.* **2.** to move very fast. *Watch the car zoom past the house.*